I'M COMING
OUT

OF THIS

Dr. John R. Adolph

TATE PUBLISHING & *Enterprises*

Published by Tate Publishing & Enterprises, LLC
127 E. Trade Center Terrace | Mustang, Oklahoma 73064 USA
1.888.361.9473 | www.tatepublishing.com

Tate Publishing is committed to excellence in the publishing industry. The company reflects the philosophy established by the founders, based on Psalm 68:11,
"The Lord gave the word and great was the company of those who published it."

Book design copyright © 2009 by Tate Publishing, LLC. All rights reserved.
Cover concept by Christopher Kirksey
Interior design by Stefanie Rooney

Published in the United States of America

ISBN: 978-1-60799-405-3
1. Religion, Christian Life, Inspirational
2. Religion, Christian Life, General
09.06.09

DEDICATION

To my Lord and savior, Jesus Christ, who blessed me with the health and strength to develop this work and teach his holy Word to his people the world over.

To my loving and beautiful wife, Dorrie, for all of her love, understanding, encouragement, prayers, patience, commitment, and support.

To my loving children, Sumone Elizabeth and Jonathan Rayshawn, who keep me filled with excitement, vigor, and purpose.

To my parents, who taught me the value of prayer, perseverance, and hard work.

To my siblings, who have always been a steadfast support.

To both my father and mother-in-law, who have supported me in every way possible.

To my Dream Team, who thought enough of me to serve as volunteers to assist me and see this book to fruition.

To Anetra, for her time and dedication in the production of this manuscript.

To my deacons, clergy ministry, administrative staff, and church family, for their willingness to receive God's Word with open ears and earnest hearts, and for all of their prayers and contributions.

To my friends, who have encouraged me along the way.

TABLE OF CONTENTS

PREFACE

Without a doubt, one of the greatest apostles to ever live was the man from Tarsus, the Apostle Paul. His writings make up about two-thirds of the New Testament canon. The impact and influence of his writings are monumental in the life of the church, second only to the teachings of Jesus Christ given to us in the gospels. The letters written to the church by this murderer-turned-missionary consists of a delicate blend that synergizes the doctrines of the Christian faith and the duties of every believer who sincerely loves the Lord.

Imagine for a moment showing up for worship service one day at a local church and the pastor introduces a guest preacher. He is excited that the guest is one of the greatest preachers who has ever lived. Yet, you feel like Forrest Gump with a box of chocolates in your hand, you just don't know what you are about to get. The pastor gives this visiting guest preacher a grand introduction. To your surprise, the guest preacher who steps up to the podium is short in stature, has a weather beaten beard, a small hunch in his back, and a slight speech impediment. The atmosphere in the room changes and you no longer feel like you are at church. It feels like you are at a bad episode of Show Time At the Apollo. You consider tiptoeing to the nearest exit like you need to use the facilities and then making a mad dash to the parking lot before the madness starts.

Just before you start to move, you realize that this is no ordinary preacher. It is the Apostle Paul and he has made his way into your life to share a word from the Lord. What would that word be? What do you think that Paul would say? What passage would he preach from? What would his subject be? What would he teach? How would he teach it? Would his message address the culture? Would it be beneficial to you?

This is where the pulse of this book is found. This book is not meant to be a commentary on the book of Philippians, though it contains vast comments on the letter. It is not meant to be a systematic treatise on Paul's writings, though it embraces the doctrines of the great apostle. It is not meant to be a deep theological exposition of the book of Philippians, though it contains exposition. Neither is it just a collection of sermons put in book form for the purpose of exhortation, though its contents are encouraging. This book is designed to be the first segment of a contemporary dialogue with the current culture from Paul's letter to the church at Philippi.

It is my firm belief that if Paul had to stand and give the morning message to you, the text would come from one of the most personal letters that he had ever written—a letter written to a small, yet faithful group of believers located in the seaport town of Philippi. I believe that his subject for the day would be culturally thought provoking, intellectually stimulating, spiritually liberating, and rooted in the redemptive healing that only comes to us through the person of Jesus Christ. In my heart I believe Paul would simply stand at the mike and say to us, "I'm coming out of this!"

In order to benefit most from the lessons shared in this work, get your Bible and read the first chapter of Philippians in its entirety. Then, start reading the contemporary dialogue given in this work. It is my sincere petition to God that the exposition, explanation, and illustrations given in each chapter will feed and inspire your spirit as you journey with Jesus Christ through time to eternity.

IT'S NOT OVER; IT'S JUST HALFTIME!

> Paul and Timotheus, the servants of Jesus Christ, to all the saints in Christ Jesus which are at Philippi, with the bishops and deacons: Grace be unto you, and peace, from God our Father, and from the Lord Jesus Christ.
>
> Philippians 1:1–2, KJV

While in London, I picked up a USA Today and noticed that Warren Moon, famed quarterback from the Houston Oilers, had become the first African American to be placed in the Hall of Fame as a quarterback. As the brisk, cool winds whipped through the window, I sat thinking on this matter while I sought rest from a long day. I quickly remembered the first time I had the chance to watch Moon play in person. It was the fall of 1985 and the Oilers were in the playoffs. They were heavily matched and highly favored against the weak and fragile Cincinnati

Bengals. If that wasn't enough to bolster their confidence, the Oilers had the home-field advantage in the Astrodome. The game was supposed to be a blow out. Texas Southern University's Ocean of Soul Marching Band was there to perform at halftime, and I had my tuba in my hand.

The stadium was packed. The atmosphere was electrifying. Columbia blue and white filled the stands. The cheerleaders were cheering and fans were screaming. It was time to get the party started. However, somebody forgot to tell Cincinnati that they were supposed to lose. They won the coin toss and elected to receive. The kick off went well until a young man caught the ball on his own three yard line and ran it all the way back for a touchdown. It was the first play of the game, and the score was already seven to zero, in favor of Cincinnati. Okay, that was luck, right? Warren Moon took the field and his first pass was picked off and returned for another touchdown, fourteen to zero Cincinnati. A hush fell over the crowd. On the next Bengals' possession, they received the ball and drove it all the way down the field allowing the clock to slowly tick away. Unfortunately, the Bengals' efficiency caused the Oilers to look like a dysfunctional college team with a bad coach and a sorry playbook. Cincinnati held a huge margin against the Oilers, as the score was now twenty-one to zero. Just before the end of the second quarter, one of the oldest plays in the book, a flee flicker, worked like magic. The halftime score was 28–0. People were disgusted. Even the cheerleaders had an attitude as if to say, "I put on all of this makeup for nothing!" It was time for the band to come down out of the stands to perform.

It was at that time that I heard it. A middle-aged woman was sitting next to a man who appeared to be semi-inebriated. She said to him, "Honey, the team is leaving the field and the game is over! Let's go. This was a waste of money and a waste of time!"

The man stood there with a beer in his hand and one too many already in his system as he responded, "Woman, don't be crazy! Our team is just getting warmed up. They just wanted to see what the Bengals had to throw at them, that's all! Bum is about to change his game plan and things are about to get good! Oh no, it's not over; it's just halftime!"

People really have it bad. We have a habit of writing people off when things don't look like they are going to work out. Has it ever happened to you? Has there ever been a time where your current condition did not look so hot and there were those near you that wrote you off before the game was over? If this has happened to you, just know that you are not alone. I believe that the overwhelming contention made throughout Paul's letter is simple yet profound. Here is the one idea that is made clear: Never let the current condition of your today determine what your tomorrow looks like. God has a habit of turning things around! Here's the announcement of joy, strength, and power that comes from this wonderful letter to the people of God who love the Lord Jesus Christ, "It's not over; it's just halftime!"

It is in the book of Philippians that we encounter that great apostle who was born out of due season, our gospel globe-trotter, Paul, and his side-kick from Lystra, Timothy. Paul is writing to a small group of faithful believers located in a Roman colony that bears the name Philippi. From the outside, the game looks bleak. The aged apostle is held captive in a Neronian jail awaiting his trial and probable execution. There are those of the faith who are talking negatively about him, hoping to add affliction to his bonds. At the same time, there are others who love him but are timid in nature. It appears that Paul is out for the season, and so is this newly formed religious sect called Christians. However, a mistake was made. They let Paul run off the field and get a chalkboard. As he wrote, out popped a mind-blowing game plan for this young Philippian team.

Paul comes out with a playbook whose watchword is joy! He opens the letter by gathering his team around him at the half to give them instructions. He says, "Epaphroditus is back on his feet and Timothy is ready to go. Our opposition thinks that the game is over, but it's just halftime and the victory is ours. Put your hands in and shout victory on three! One, two, three … victory!" The huddle breaks and the letter commences!

The message that Paul's letter conveyed to the Philippians is the same message that he has for us today. It is for people who have had a rough time and have had others write you off. This letter is for the student who is headed back to school after a tough year last year and some people think that this year will just be a repeat of last year. This is for the administrator that was treated unfairly and whose peers think that their career is over. It is for the couple whose marriage is really struggling and it is starting to seem as if all is lost. This is for the saint who is physically ill and the prognosis of their condition looks bleak. It is for the believer who has suffered a death in the family and feels like they just cannot go on. This letter is for the seasoned saint whose skin is wrinkled and some people think that because they are older they are washed up. Here's the great news of this letter—the news that brings healing and wholeness—it's not over; it's just halftime! It's time for you to rethink your victory, revisit your purpose, and come out with your head up, ready to move forward! I know you are thinking, *All of this sounds great, but what should I do to turn things around in my life?* That very question is the core study of this chapter. Paul makes it clear that if you are going to turn things around there are some things that are required in order to bring it to fruition. Here's what you must have.

• • •

A Friend That's Saved

Paul and Timotheus, the servants of Jesus Christ ...
Phil. 1:1a

I hate to be the bearer of bad news, but let me give it to you straight—most of the people that you think are authentic friends in your life aren't. They are fair weather friends at best. As long as your life is going good, they are there. But let trouble come. Fall down. Get sick. Get into trouble. Mess something up. I assure you, you will quickly discover just how real they are.

What we discover about Paul is that in his half-time episode, he has at least one real friend. Paul is in jail and that is when Timothy appears. Did you hear that? Did you get it? Paul is in jail, he is in trouble, things are not going well, and Timothy is present! Now, that's a real friend. In fact, Timothy is so close to Paul that it is probable that it is Timothy who is actually dictating this letter. Paul helps us understand the glue that holds this relationship together. They are both *servants* of Christ Jesus. The Greek word for servant is *duolos*. It means to be a slave. Further, it means to be a slave even after you have been freed. It is where a slave is released, but his master has been so good to him that he goes to the gate of the city and says, "This is my master forever." To make things better, look at whom these two are serving together: Jesus Christ. He is the Son of the living God. He is their Master, Servant, and their Lord.

I have always been taught that the company we keep defines us. If we run with wolves, we will learn to howl. My grandmother put it in this fashion: "If you lay with dogs, you will get fleas." But if you run with people who know how to stand when things get tough, pray when things seem impossible, and press on when things seem impermeable, then you have a friend, a friend indeed.

Jesus Christ told his disciples, "Henceforth, I call you not servants; for the servant knoweth not what his lord doeth: but I have called you friends; for all things that I have heard of my Father I have made known unto you" (John 15:15). We also find in 1 Samuel 19:1–7, that when David was in hot water, Jonathan was his friend and stood by him. Even when Jonathan's father, Saul, wanted to kill David, Jonathan was his friend; and he hung in there with him.

I recently met a young lady that faithfully attends the church I pastor. She has been delivered from drugs and alcohol for twelve years. When I asked her how she did it, she smiled and said, "Well, first I had to realize that I could do bad all by myself, and some folks I had near me were not helping me. Secondly, I discovered that Jesus was really real! I had heard about him. I had even sung songs about him. But this time, I tried him for myself. Thirdly, I had one good friend that would stick with me no matter how tough things got for me. Without my friend I would not have made it!"

Has God ever done it for you? Has he ever providentially placed a person in your life when things were going rough just to tell you to hold on? It is his way of letting you know that it is not over; it's just halftime!

. . .

A Fellowship That's Saturated

... to all the saints in Christ Jesus which are at Philippi, with the bishops and deacons.

Phil. 1:1b

Listen, if you are making some halftime adjustments in your life, an ordinary church fellowship will not do. You must have a supernatural fellowship where God is worshipped, miracles happen, prayers are heard, sinners are saved, the gospel is preached, demons are removed, and lives are changed. Just any church will not do. If you are going to see a change in your life, you will need to be near a fellowship of believers that love the Lord, recognize the presence of the Holy Spirit, and understand the divine purpose of the church of the living God. Not the presence of an ordinary church, but an extraordinary one. A body of believers that are organized so that the Holy Spirit has free course, the word of God is honored and obeyed, and the people of God actually *do* what the scriptures say and not just sit in small groups having discussions about what they feel the Bible has said.

That's the picture Paul paints for us regarding the church at Philippi. No, they are not perfect, but thank

God they are not like the church in Corinth either. They may not be large in number, but they are great at doing the will of God. Paul writes to this church in Philippi and he calls them "saints" who are with the "bishops and deacons." Here's what's supernatural. Saints are not dead believers who are resting from their labor as some suppose. To the contrary, they are redeemed believers who were sinners but have been saved by grace. That is why Paul mentioned they are "in Christ Jesus." This entire idea suggests one thing and one thing only, saved by grace alone through the person of Jesus Christ alone!

The next phrase is where we see the order, structure, and the power base in a local church. In Greek it is *episkopos kai diakonos,* "bishops and deacons" Philippians 1:1b. Bishop means to oversee, to set in place, and to keep order. The concept of deacon is not mentioned without being in conjunction with the bishop, simply because deacons are a pastoral office. Churches do not have deacons; bishops have deacons. The word *diakonos* in general means to serve but specifically it means to get one's hands dirty. Thus, deacons are those believers that are basically chief servants of the church whose job is to assist the bishop by serving the people.

Now here is where we find the problem. In most church settings the Holy Spirit can not move freely through the body of Christ because saints are living like sinners, bishops are often filled with a sense of arrogance and want to be worshipped, and deacons stop serving so they can become governing boards that seek both power and control within local assemblies. Thus, the end result is a form of religion but no real spiritual power. In either case, the body that was saved to serve ends up sick and weak. When saints live in sin, it's like a clot in the leg. When deacons become boards and refuse to serve, it's like a clot to the lung. In the medical field they call this an embolism. When the overseer or bishop has lost his mind and forgets that he is not the redeemer, and that he too has been redeemed, it is like a clot to the brain and it can cause death.

But when things are in order! When saints live right, bishops oversee the flock with integrity, and deacons serve with a sense of passion and purpose, the person of the Holy Spirit moves through the church, and awesome things happen! If you want to see God move mightily in the midst of people, just create an environment where the Holy Spirit can lead the church without interference from outside ideas that merely sound good but lack substance. This is exactly what took place in Acts when the early church had its beginning. In fact, the book of Acts should never be called "Acts of the Apostles." It should be "Acts of the Holy Spirit." It was the Holy Spirit at work in his church that we have recorded on those pages. In Acts, signs and wonders were the norm, healing and miracles happened all of the time, the church prayed with fervor and faith, and the Holy Ghost was in charge of every meeting (Acts 5). The end result was a fellowship that was saturated with Holy Ghost power that was life transforming. Witnessing, healing, and blessings were the order of the day.

A few years ago, a young man joined our church, and his purpose for uniting with our fellowship was unique, to say the least. He was diagnosed as being HIV-positive and decided to join the church, not so that he could find the Lord Jesus Christ and be saved, but so that when he died he would have a nice, dignified church edifice to have his funeral. Well, it has been a few years now and he is still alive! He has received salvation through the finished work of Jesus Christ on the cross, and God is healing his body one day at a time. If you ask him how he feels, he often replies in this fashion: "I'm getting better every day." If you ask him what happened to him, he will tell you, "The Lord led me to a church that was saturated with Holy Ghost power." Halftime ends when you get into a fellowship that will say yes to God's word and yes to God's will!

• • •

A Fuel That Strengthens

Grace be unto you, and peace …

Phil. 1:2a

A car can only go so far before it needs to be refueled. A lawn mower can only cut so much grass before it will need more gas. A saint can only go so far without stopping and gaining more strength for the journey that lies ahead. Here's the truth: all of us run low from time-to-time and need a refill. In fact, some of you reading this book right now are running low. Some saints run low on peace in their lives, and yet others can run low on their personal prayer lives. But, if you are going to come out fighting, you must get refueled. Here's how you do it! Paul says, "Grace be unto you, and peace" (Phil. 1:2a).

These words are not just an integral part of a traditional greeting used by Paul, but they are the fuel that energizes the soul of anyone who loves the Lord and seeks to serve him faithfully. Grace (*charis*) deals with God's unmerited favor he shows toward you, and peace (*iraynay*) deals with God's presence that flows from you. Grace says, "God did it for me even though I did not deserve it." Peace says, "Whatever God does in my life, I trust him; and I am fine with it because I know he has my best interest at heart." Thus, there is an interconnectedness that exists between grace and peace that simply suggests that the more grace you receive the more peace you should possess.

If you ever want to brighten your day and refuel your soul, find a nice, quiet spot and seriously consider all of the grace that God has bestowed upon your life thus far. Do your very best to earnestly consider all that the Lord has done for you. Are you thinking yet? Think of how lost you were before meeting the Lord. Think of his perfect sacrifice. Think of his multifaceted blessings that he has bestowed upon your life. When you pause to consider just how good the Lord has been, it refuels your heart; and the comfort that exudes from you once you have considered the grace of God is the peace of God. You cannot have one without the other. In fact, when Paul mentions "grace ... and peace" it forms a wonderful combination of inner strength that can only come from the Lord. Get this, grace goes in and peace comes out!

One of my favorite stories in the scriptures is that of the great Prophet Elijah recorded in 1 Kings 19:9–18. In this story the great prophet and man of God is hiding in a cave, covered by a spirit that could very easily be seen as depression. God met him where he was and simply reminded him that he was not alone and that he had more work to do. Okay, retranslation my way: God met him while he was stuck in a rut running the wrong direction and simply reminded him of just how great the Lord had been to him. He helped him get back up on his feet and continue moving forward in the face of his enemies. That's grace and peace! Grace found him and peace is what he had when he left the cave.

Not long ago I met a young, dynamic pastor who was responsible for leading a congregation of nearly 17,000 believers. I asked him how he managed to keep all of those people returning each week for worship to hear him declare the word of the living God, and his answer floored me. He said, "Oh, that's the easy part. I just remind them of how gracious the Lord has been to them and they come back the next week ready for me to remind them once again!" In essence, what he was saying was that people often run empty and return to the house of God to be refueled.

. . .

A Faith That's Solid

> ... from God our Father and the Lord Jesus Christ.
> Phil. 1:2b

Here's some solid advice that will work when it is halftime in your life—stick to the faith in the Lord that has worked for you to get you where you are right now. Stick to your bread and butter. After halftime there is no time for trick plays, new game plans that have never worked before, or ideas that come from unknown and unfamiliar sources. Get to the game plan that is the core of Christianity. Stick with the God who is one in essence and triune in personality! Stay faithful to the God who is our Father and Jesus Christ, his Son. Just think of it, have they ever let you down before? Be encouraged by the fact that his résumé says that he is able to help you when no one else can.

God in this segment of the verse is characterized as being "our Father." By this, Paul means that God is our source. God alone is the one who shapes our destiny, handles our future, and controls our fate. Jesus is then described as being "our Lord." The apostle means that Jesus is our *kurios:* our controller. Jesus is the one who is responsible for controlling every element of your life from start to finish. In conjunction with being Lord, he is also Christ. He is the promised Messiah who is the sum total of who God is, in the flesh! For Jesus Christ is both Lord and Christ of every saved soul. Faith in him will never ever fail you, no matter where you are in life.

Well, Bumb Philips, head coach of the Houston Oilers, hit the field after the half with his team's bread and butter in mind. They were about to get back to the game plan that got them to the playoffs to begin with. In fact, Moon did not throw many more passes at all. They put the ball in the hands of Earl Campbell, a man they called the "Tyler Rose." His thighs were a massive thirty-three inches in diameter. He rushed for a record setting 338 yards in one half of football, setting a new league record. He scored five rushing touchdowns and he won their game! The Bengals would knock him down and it would take him forever to get up, but when he did he was unstoppable. You see, the team won the game on the back of just one man that simply refused to stay down. In a nutshell, the same is true for you too.

No, we do not have a Tyler Rose, but we do have a Rose of Sharon. We do not have a running back with thirty-three inch thighs, but we do have a redeemer who lived thirty- three years on the earth. Yes, he was knocked down by opposing forces on Calvary, and it took him a while to get up. In fact, he stayed in a grave for three days, but when he rose, he got up with all power in his hand! On his back alone we have won the game. His name is Jesus Christ, Son of the living God. With the Lord on your side, your game is not over. You may have to make some halftime adjustments, but keep the ball in his hands and he will never fail you. Remember, your game is not over; it's just halftime!

PARDON OUR MESS; WE'RE UNDER CONSTRUCTION AND MAKING SOME IMPROVEMENTS

> I thank my God upon every remembrance of you, Always in every prayer of mine for you all making request with joy, For your fellowship in the gospel from the first day until now; Being confident of this very thing, that he which hath begun a good work in you will perform it until the day of Jesus Christ.
>
> Phil. 1:3–6

It was the summer of 1999 and I needed some rest from ministry work. I had been working overtime at the church. To make matters worse, I had been attending graduate school in Houston, Texas, and was just about to graduate. In short, I had been a graduate student for seven long years. I was excited about everything that God was doing in my life, but I was tired. Quite honestly, *exhausted* may be a better term for me to use. It was then that Deacon W.H. Taft encouraged me to take a vacation. Deacon Taft was 88 years old at the time, and with great wisdom he told me the only way to become an old man was to learn how to master moderation. He often exclaimed with vigor that too much of anything was bad for you, and that included working at the church. So, I took a break.

I went home and asked my wonderful wife, Dorrie, where she would like to go. I wanted her to tell me some place we had never been before. She told me with no reservation, "Honey, I want to go to Aruba!" Aruba? What happened to Florida? What's wrong with Jamaica? Aruba? Where is that? I had never heard of Aruba, but my foot was now in my mouth and I had to follow through on the deal. I found a map and I located this tiny island off the coast of Venezuela. Many thoughts crossed my mind at the time. Thoughts like, *Why didn't I just choose a simple place to visit that would have been cheap, but nice, and within the constraints of my stingy budget, and then surprise her with a trip? Why can't we just take a simple cruise for three days and come home? Is this vacation going to put me in the poor house? Will I need an "I will work for food" sign after this vacation?* Of the numerous thoughts that crossed my mind, none of them were pleasant. In fact, I remember praying my emergency request prayer that same day. It is simple and flows like this: "Help me, Lord! Help me!"

Finally, I contacted a travel agent and she told me the costs for this trip, and to the best of my recollection, a tear literally trickled from my eye. Trust me; it was not a tear of joy. Okay, let me admit it openly, I am conservative. All right—I'll say what I mean and mean what I say here—I am cheap. Don't judge me, because some of you are on the conservative side also. But thank God, he did it for me! We paid for the trip and made our way to Aruba; however, the only way to get there was to spend one night in the gorgeous city of San Juan, Puerto Rico.

The plane landed safely and we were filled with an air of excitement. We got off the plane with our hotel reservations and travel guide in hand. Yes, we looked like tourists that were as lost as a golf ball in high weeds. However, our excitement came to a slow halt when we started walking through the airport. Things were a mess. Dust was everywhere, the lights were dim, and things didn't look so hot. We managed to get our bags and make our way to the taxi stand to get a ride to the hotel, but just before we hit the exit door there was a huge sign that left a life long impression on me. The sign read, "Please pardon our mess; we're under construction and making some improvements." Wow, what a concept! It not only stuck with me the entire time we were vacationing, but it preached to me. That sign would pop up on the screen of my mind while we were shopping for souvenirs. (Great timing for a conservative brother, right?) I would wake up and see that sign. I would take a nap and see that sign in my sleep.

That expression resonated within me because, like that airport, none of us are completed projects yet. There are some believers who will make you think that they are completed and perfect, flawless and without sin. But I caution you, do not let them fool you. Not one of us living on earth has it all together. In fact, we should all have lime green T-shirts with that slogan from the airport on it and wear them once or twice a week. "Please pardon our mess; we're under construction and making some improvements." Yes, I said lime green! No one would miss you. Wear it for your judgmental co-workers who are quick to say things like, "And you call yourself a Christian," every time they see you make a mistake. Wear it for really religious do-gooders who think that they never make a mistake. Wear it for your unsaved family members who wait for you to do or say anything that just seems a little off kilter so that they can point a finger. I love it! "Please pardon our mess; we're under construction and making some improvements."

As this epistle opens, it is evident that this is another Pauline masterpiece. What I love about it is that in the core of this passage of scripture, Paul makes the sign from Puerto Rico a reality for every Christian. As the great apostle writes to this Philippian church, he opens by making it clear that he is praying for them. He also mentions that for him, the gospel and the Philippians'partnership with him in it means a great deal. He even goes as far as to call them "his joy." But, Paul says he is "confident that he which hath begun a good work in you will perform it until the day of Jesus Christ." A modern day translation of this would simply be, "Please pardon our mess; we're under construction and making some improvements."

Let me ask a rather probing question. Have you studied yourself well enough to know that you have some real issues that God needs to work on for you? I hope that your answer was a swift "yes," because if not, it means that you have been too busy examining the faults and mishaps of others. The real truth of the matter is this: we are not completed projects yet. However, we have a great general contractor who has a copy of the master plan in his hand, and he is not done with us just yet. He is still working to perfect us, shape us, mature us, and mold us into the image of his only begotten Son! While we are in that process, we can boldly declare with a sense of freedom: "Please pardon our mess; we're under construction and making some improvements." Meanwhile, what should we know about the Lord and the work he is doing on us as believers in the faith?

• • •

The Contractor Knows What He Is Doing

I thank my God upon every remembrance of you, Always in every prayer of mine for you all making request with joy, For your fellowship in the gospel from the first day until now; Being confident of this very thing...

Phil. 1:3–6

I live in Beaumont, Texas, which is located on the Gulf Coast. In the fall of 2005, we were hit by the gale force hurricane winds of Rita that belted our region, leaving people homeless, hurt, and confused. The storm caused an enormous amount of property damage. During this season of my life, I learned that if you are going to repair a home or some damaged property, you need a contractor who really knows what he is doing. You see, a cheap contractor will do cheap work. An ignorant contractor will do tacky work. But a great contractor will do great work. In short, I learned that if you are going to make some improvements, you have to be careful who you let work on your project.

The same holds true for us as saints in the Lord Jesus Christ. Here's a word of caution to you, and it is worth repeating. Be careful whom you let work on your project! Let me share with you what I mean. Have you ever had somebody tell you how to construct your life, but when you look at theirs it is a complete mess? Here's good old common sense. If their advice is so good, why is their life a total mess? Before they go to work on your life, let them get their own stuff in order. Hear this please: the only licensed and bonded contractor in the world suitable for working on your life is God!

Paul says "being confident ... that he." The word confident in Greek is *pitho*. It means to be pushed to the edge of a cliff. The idea here is phenomenal! Through contemporary interpretation we could contend that if Paul were a betting man then pitho would translate like this: I am willing to put all of my chips on this one thing. It would be his way of saying, "I am sure that God will not fail me and I would be willing to risk it all to prove it." He is confident! Confident in *what* you ask? Paul is confident that the contractor of his soul knows what he is doing with his life and the lives of his people whom he died to save from sin.

The age in which we now live has been characterized by many as the age of hopelessness and brokenness. This is because of the moral collapse we are witnessing. Things seem to be spiraling downwards. Nevertheless, the great news of the day is this: when we are at our worst, God is at his best! As the contractor of our lives, he is both competent and qualified to heal what is sick and mend what is broken.

Just think about it for a moment. The Lord has been mending and repairing people since time began. David was guilty of extortion, but he had a great contractor. Abraham was a liar, but he had a great contractor. Jeremiah was a weeping prophet, but even he introduced us to the potter's house. Here's the bottom line—God knows what he is doing with us and we can be confident in him and his work.

Friday, August 11, 2006, is a day I will never forget. It was a day when God let me see something that I had never witnessed before in my life. The prison ministry of our church conducted a week-long crusade in the Gist Unit in Jefferson County, Texas. For four nights we worshipped the Lord, shared the gospel of Jesus Christ, and prayed for the men there who needed a new contractor in their lives. On the fifth night, we had a baptismal and communion service for those men that accepted Jesus Christ as their personal Lord and Savior during the revival. It was that night that it happened. We baptized 104 men—men that had been shot, stabbed, tattooed, and of course, had made mistakes and needed redemption. It was one of the most exciting moments of my life! I saw men with huge muscles and chiseled bodies weep like little children as they surrendered their lives to the one general contractor of the universe, Jesus Christ. He is the maker and creator of this world and the world to come. I knew that as they were baptized they were confident that he alone could save them.

• • •

You Are His Project

... he which hath begun a good work in you ... "

Phil. 1: 6b

I was raised around older believers that had strong faith in God. I would listen to them talk and discuss the ideals of the Christian faith. One of the things that I often heard them say over and over again, and now holds true for me, is the saying, "The Lord has brought me a mighty long way!" Take a moment and briefly review your personal pilgrimage with the Lord. Just pause for a moment and think. Can you say the same? Has the Lord brought you a long way in your life too? If you know the Lord like I do, your testimony may not be identical to mine but we may share this one sentiment together: "When I look at what my life was like before encountering the saving grace of Jesus Christ and the realness of a steadfast relationship with him through his finished work on the cross, I can truthfully say that the Lord has brought me a mighty long way." But why has God done this for us? The answer here is awesome. We are his personal projects, his construction site, if you will.

Paul says it like this: "he which hath begun a good work in you." The idea here is overwhelming. If you are a born-again believer in Jesus Christ, you are the construction site of God. He is doing a work in your life and it is a good one. The word "begun" used by Paul here is the term *enarchomai,* which means, the work got started before you ever knew that the work was needed! The apostle calls the work a "good work." It is good for two reasons. First of all, it is good because God is doing it himself. God would never entrust this kind of work to anyone. And secondly, he is still working right now and will continue to do so until we are completed projects.

In Ephesians 2:10 we find these words, "For we are his workmanship, created in Christ Jesus unto good works which God hath before ordained that we should walk in them." The concept here is wonderful. The word workmanship (*poiema*) literally meant the place of construction. It was used to describe a poet constructing a beautiful poem or a painter with a dynamic drawing on a canvas. It even referred to the elaborate construction of a temple. Regardless of the illustration, the idea was awesome because it displays the fact that the person doing the work is the creator and the object being worked on is the creation. When the creator has completed work on the creation, the creation will be the glory of the creator. This is the exciting news that Paul is delivering. You are the construction site of almighty God the creator and he is still at work in your life as his greatest creation. He is your contractor, and what he is doing in your life, now that you are aware of it and even before you knew anything about it, was a good work.

Calvin Cuther is an artist from Atlanta, Georgia, who does excellent African American portraits.

They are stunning in detail and breathtaking in cultural significance. I love his work. My wife and I have his paintings all over our home. The problem with his work arises when you watch him draw his masterpieces. He moves slowly. Sometimes the canvas looks like a two-year-old had a field day with finger paint. But no matter what it looks like during the process, each time he finishes a project, it turns out great. You see, Calvin knows from the beginning what his project will be, so he develops a good work! Now, if Calvin can do that on his canvas with a painting, what about what God is doing on the canvas of your life? You are his construction site, and he has started and is continuing to work on you until the masterpiece is completed.

• • •

He Will Finish The Job

... will perform it until the day of Christ.

Phil. 1:6c

During our reconstruction period in the city of Beaumont following Hurricane Rita, we saw it quite a bit, and it was seriously frustrating. What did we see, you ask? Contractors would start a project but would not finish the job. It was terrible. A floor partially repaired. A wall with only half of the sheet rock replaced. A ceiling that was only half repaired and produced even more leaks. It was frustrating! There's nothing worse than a contractor that will not finish the job. I visited a friend one day who had a contractor who left his job undone. I couldn't help but smile. He asked me what I found so amusing about his unfinished work, and I replied, "Philippians 1:6." You see, God does not start a project that he does not complete. If he starts it, he will finish it every time.

Here's what the latter part of verse six says: "he will perform it until the day of Christ." The word "perform" is in the future, active, indicative tense. In a nutshell, it means the job is already completed. It is a done deal! For God, to start is to finish. Some people are good at half doing things, but God never has half done anything! He does the whole thing or he does nothing at all.

Think of it for a moment. God is our creator, but did he half create the earth? He brought Moses through the Red Sea, but did he leave a few of his people behind? And when he died on the cross did he half do the job? Did he partially hang on the cross? Did he die just a little bit? No! He did the job completely. He paid the price for our sins once and for all. He rose once and for all! The Lord never ever does a partial job. He completes the tasks that he starts.

The Robinsons were having their home built and were very excited. However, I noticed that Sister Pam was buying a lot of items before the home was actually finished. I decided to play the devil's advocate on this one and asked her why she was buying all of this stuff when the house was not even finished yet. Something could go wrong and the house could end up not being completed. Even while I spoke, she smiled and shook her head as if to say, "Not a fat chance." She confidently replied, "Before we got started with this project I checked the contractor's background. He has never had a job that he did not finish. I am getting my stuff right now because my house is already done." Did you get it? Her contractor had a track record of finishing projects. That's what Paul is saying here, and it is shouting news for those that really love the Lord. God will finish the work that he has started in us!

Well, our trip to the island of Aruba was like a dream come true. Just like we had to stop in San Juan on the outbound trip, we had to return the same way to get home. But this time the airport was different. In just seven days, things went from being a total mess to being one of the most beautiful airports I had ever seen. It was gorgeous. I looked for my sign. You know, the one that read, "Please pardon our mess; we're under construction and making some improvements," but I could not find it. It was gone. It was then that it hit me. Once the work was completed, the sign was no longer needed. The contractor took care of business and completed his job.

In my heart this was shouting news, because the same holds true for those of us who know the Lord and believe. One of these days we will be completed projects, because our contractor does not start a job that he does not finish. Right now we are simply under construction and the master himself is at work in us, molding us into the image of his Son, Jesus Christ!

WHEN THE ENEMY STRIKES

Even as it is meet for me to think this of you all, because I have you in my heart; inasmuch as both in my bonds, and in the defense and confirmation of the gospel, ye all are partakers of my grace. For God is my record, how greatly I long after you all in the bowels of Jesus Christ. And this I pray, that your love may abound yet more and more in knowledge and in all judgment; That ye may approve things that are excellent; that ye may be sincere and without offence till the day of Christ; Being filled with the fruits of righteousness, which are by Jesus Christ, unto the glory and praise of God.

Phil. 1:7–11

I t happens all of a sudden. It happens so quickly, in most cases, that you hardly have time to brace yourself for the attack. It can happen on a day when there is not a cloud in the sky, and all seems well; and it can happen on a dark, wet, and rainy day. It does happen, and it happens to sincere Christian people everyday. The enemy strikes! Contrary to popular opinion, real Christians are targets for our adversary, the devil. The Apostle Peter describes him, saying, "a roaring lion, walketh about, seeking whom he may devour." Jesus calls him, "the thief who cometh but for to steal, kill, and destroy" (John 10:10a). He is a real enemy; and he strikes often and, in most instances, with no warning at all.

It happened to native Houstonian Valarie Gibson. Val, as she is affectionately called by her family and friends, is a born-again believer in the Lord Jesus Christ. She was raised and reared by Christian parents who taught her and her siblings the moral values and virtues of the Christian faith. Val was gainfully employed with a local school district in the Houston area. She worked within the district handling critical fiduciary matters, and might I add, she was excellent at it. In fact, all of her job reviews were wonderful, simply because she did her job with great effectiveness and efficiency. However, all of a sudden she found herself under enemy attack.

One day while the sun was shining and all appeared to be well, the Federal Bureau of Investigation walked into her office and asked her a series of questions regarding a particular check. She had some knowledge of it, but like other district disbursements, it too was handled with the same written procedure and protocol. She answered all of their questions and she thought that the ordeal was over. Little did she know, the two-year train ride through the valley of difficulty and heartache was just beginning. Within a few hours, she found herself handcuffed. They took all of her personal belongings, strip-searched her, and placed her in jail until she could be bonded out.

Can you imagine a day like this happening in your life? Val was in jail, charged with fraud, theft, and other charges, just to name a few. She wept; she was hurt, embarrassed, humiliated, and angry. She was living a nightmare! Her family gathered around her. People of faith who knew her and her background started praying. As she settled down, she realized that this was an attack of the enemy.

Things like this don't just happen to Val. They can happen to anyone who loves the Lord and is saved through the cross of Jesus Christ. It is nothing more than an example of when the enemy strikes. Has it ever happened to you before? Have you ever had a phone call change your life? Have you ever had a child rebel for no reason? Have you ever been hit by a drunk driver that you never saw coming? Have you ever returned home from a hard day's work only to find your front door open and your house a mess due to burglary? Have you ever had attacks launched at you like fiery missiles from the enemy's camp that altered your life forever? Have you ever had a spouse walk into the room, and without warning or reason, decide that they just do not want to be married anymore?

Have you ever been terminated from your job for no reason at all? The enemy has a way of attacking all of us. It could happen to any of us.

As we read this letter that Paul is writing from Philippi, this is exactly what is going on in his life. This letter is called a prison epistle. This is due to the fact that Paul is writing it while under house arrest with Nero on the throne. Now if you know nothing about Nero, let me say quickly that he was a crazy man, a megalomaniac. He was a ruthless leader that sought to make the lives of Christians a living hell. He was an instrument of the devil. Antiquity says that he would place Christians in huge stadiums and have them eaten alive by man-eating beasts and animals. This was a form of entertainment. He was ruthless! Nero would take the body of a Christian, strap it to a huge post, and pour flammable liquid over the body. He would light it and use the burning corpse to light up his banquet hall while he ate dinner. He was a demon-possessed man.

Paul finds himself in prison with this kind of a leader on the throne, but what has he done wrong? Is he guilty of breaking the law? No. Has he robbed, killed, murdered, stolen, or committed any kind of crime? No. Perhaps he is guilty of not paying tribute taxes, holding parades without a permit, or even treason against the Roman Empire. The answer again is no. He has been imprisoned for declaring the wonderful news about Jesus Christ who has risen from the dead and is Lord! In short, he is under enemy attack.

Now here is the real truth. If the enemy will tempt Jesus in the wilderness (Matt. 4:1–8), if he will test Job (Job 1), and if he will falsely imprison Paul, you should know that you are not exempt from the heartaches that he causes in life. If you have not already seen him attack your life, you should prepare for the day that will come when the enemy strikes! What we must focus on for this chapter is what you need in place when the enemy strikes.

· · ·

Praying People That Have Your Best Interest At Heart

> Even as it is meet for me to think this of you all, because I have you in my heart; inasmuch as both in my bonds, and in the defense and confirmation of the gospel, ye all are partakers of my grace. For God is my record, how greatly I long after you all in the bowels of Jesus Christ.
>
> Phil. 1:7–8

When I was a younger believer I would ask everyone I knew to pray for me. However, I no longer do that. In fact, let me personally warn you against such. Here's why. Everybody that's praying for you may not have your best interest at heart. There are some people who possess secret spirits of jealousy, envy, and hatred for you; and many times you are completely oblivious to it. The end result is a person that will smile in your face, stab you in your back, and cause havoc in your life. Everyone does not want to see you blessed, healed, delivered, set free, and strong. You have to be careful about asking everybody to pray for you. You need people to pray for you that have your best interest at heart.

Allow me to retranslate what Paul is saying, "I know the enemy is really busy, and I can not get to you personally, but I have been lifting you in my prayers privately." The words are deep and very meaningful in verses 7 and 8. The apostle says, "I think of you all, because I have you in my heart." He goes even deeper when he says that he "long[s] after you all in the *bowels* of Jesus Christ." The Greek word here for bowels is *splang-non*. We borrow our word spleen from it. It refers to the vital organs of the upper torso. We would translate it like this: "I have your best interest at heart."

The great thing about prayer is that it, like God, is not bound by spatial limitations. With this, I mean that you do not need to be near a person to pray earnestly for them. All you really need is to have their best interest in your soul, and take it to the Lord on their behalf; God will do the rest. When you consider Christian principles like this, it is a fact that many of us are still living on the prayers of those who prayed for us before we could pray for ourselves. Many of you reading this book have been blessed because of prayers that were prayed for you way back when. These prayers were prayed for you to the Lord and had your best interest at heart.

In the book of Exodus 39:1–14, the priestly attire was designed by the Lord. The priests who served were to wear a linen ephod made of blue, purple, and red. It was to be a beautiful garment. However, it was not designed to be pretty, but rich in significance. In the center of the priest's chest were twelve precious stones (see verse 14). There was one stone for each of the twelve tribes. It was a wonderful symbol that said this: Though the priest may not always be near the people when he was offering sacrifices and making intercessions, he had their best interest on his heart. Therefore, distance did not matter at all.

Not long ago, during a conference at the church, a sister was so excited to get into the building that she left her keys on the front seat of her car. She got out of the car and picked up her umbrella and purse but left her keys behind. She had called security but then realized that it was okay. She simply said, "I'll call my husband and he will open it for me." I was thinking that her husband was going to hop into his pick-up truck and ride to the church. However, that is not what happened. The lady called her husband who was at work and said, "Honey, get your keys." She continued, "I locked my keys in the car and I need you to help me open the door. Take your lock, aim it at the phone, and press the unlock button. I will aim my cell phone at the car." Her husband, who was at work, took his keys and pressed the unlock button and the woman's door popped open. She smiled, then looked at me and said, "When you are using tools like these, distance doesn't matter!" Now if distance does not matter for things like this, you should know that distance does not matter for issues of prayer. If you are going to endure an enemy strike, you need some praying people on your side that have your best interest at heart.

• • •

Powerful Principles for Spiritual Discernment

> And this I pray, that your love may abound yet more and more in knowledge and in all judgment; That ye may approve things that are excellent; that ye may be sincere and without offence till the day of Christ.
>
> Philippians 1:9–10

One of the things that the enemy is good at doing is clouding your mind. He will cause you to question if what you know is right. He does this all for the single purpose of leading you away to hurt, chaos, and even destruction. Has he ever done it to you? Be honest. He is the absolute best at getting us to do what Eve did in the Garden of Eden. He will have us go back and reexamine the instructions that God gave us, only for him to lie so that we end up confused.

As a child I heard the familiar clichés that were used by my parents. Back then they did not make much sense to me. You've heard them before. "Everything that glitters is not gold; everything that looks good to you, is not good for you; you are the company that you keep." It is so amazing how all of these little sayings hold great truth within them. It is because they offer clearly defined boundaries for spiritual discernment. You see, when encountering an enemy attack, the one thing that you must possess is the ability to discern.

Paul gives us three golden nuggets that cannot be missed if victory is going to be gained. He says, first of all, "and this I pray, that your love abound yet more and more in knowledge and all judgment." Simply put: it's not that I believe I am better than you, but I love you enough to let you know when you're wrong. He says, "I have some knowledge." A better translation of this would be to say: "I have been around the track a few times and I know what's right and what is not. I know what is holy and I know what is sinful. In short, discernment is one of my spiritual assets." Then in verse 10, he uses the phrase "approve those things which are excellent" The word approve in Greek is *dokimadzo,* and it means to test something to see if it is authentic. It was a word used in testing money to see it if was counterfeit. The big idea is that everything that looks excellent is not, but if it withstands the test, then it is approved. However, if it does not, then knowledge and judgment has given you the ability to possess the power of spiritual discernment.

One of the greatest men of the Bible had his mind clouded by poor discernment and enemy attack. If it could happen to him, it could happen to any believer. In 1 Kings 19, Elijah, has just had a great victory over the prophets of Baal on Mount Carmel. Yet when he hears the threat of Jezebel and her plans to have him killed, he runs and hides in a cave. The irony is overwhelming. He just defeated a mountain filled with men, and yet now he is on the run from one woman. The Lord appears to him to assure him that God is still faithful and has all power in his hand. God has to get Elijah up and make him move on. Why? While the man of God was in the cave, the enemy had his mind clouded, and he was in need of some serious spiritual discernment. Knowledge and judgment should have told him that if God was with him on the mountain, the same God would be with him everywhere else.

I have a good friend whose name is Randal. He is a great guy who was raised in church and loves the Lord sincerely. Randal was dating a young lady that caused him to compromise every Christian value he ever thought he had. Granted, she was beautiful, charming, fun, sweet, nice, and well rounded; but at the end of the day she was dangerous. Randal did not drink at all. He just did not believe in it. But that was before he met her. Randal did not believe in nightclubs and after parties. But that too was before he met her. Randal did not believe in fornication and living together prior to marriage. But that was before Ms. Charming turned him upside down. After a few months the relationship ended. He gathered all of his friends in his dormitory room and told us that he made a decision to stop seeing the young lady when he realized that he had forsaken everything that he ever believed in for brief moments of delight. He said, "When I was with her, she clouded my thinking, and I compromised it all." When the enemy attacks, he will cloud your mind. If he did it to Randal, he can do it to you. When the enemy attacks, spiritual discernment is a must!

• • •

Personal Prosperity Evidenced By Good Fruit

Being filled with the fruits of righteousness...

Phil. 1:11a

There is a huge secret I must share with you. If you ever want to get the devil off your back, shift your focus from fear to fruit! In short, stop looking at what you do not have and consider what you do have. I believe in the age-old philosophy that teaches that no one has everything, but everybody has something. If you are a believer in the Lord Jesus Christ, there has to be some fruit somewhere in your life. This fruit is a clear sign of God's faithfulness in your life. This concept is vitally important in combat and spiritual attacks. Here's why: The presence of fruit is the evidence of faith.

Verse eleven says, "Being filled with the fruits of righteousness." The Greek word for "filled" is the word *play-ro-o*. It means to run over the top, painting a picture of a cup that is overflowing. The idea of "righteousness" used by Paul has to do with the very character of God. Therefore, the "fruits of righteousness" means to be filled with truth, love, patience, strength, salvation, power, grace, mercy, joy, and so many other things that it is literally too much for you to contain. The awesome part about "being filled" is that it is a current action that's taking place. It is not as if you are full already; you are being filled. Get this, it is happening right now! God is filling his children every moment, every minute, and every day; and the end result of being filled is to possess the fruits of righteousness.

There's an old cliché that says, "You can tell a tree by the fruit it bears." If this old saying is true, then you know when you are in the presence of a pecan tree. The evidence of pecans will be in the nearby proximity. You know when you are near a lemon tree. The evidence of lemons will be complete proof. Likewise, you know when you are near a Christian who is in the midst of a spiritual attack, because what keeps them and holds them is the fruit of God's righteousness that comes from within them.

I love the Old Testament story of Joseph (Genesis 37). He is betrayed by his own family. He is then falsely accused by a woman for no reason at all, and as punishment for a crime he never committed, he ends up in a pit in Egypt. Joseph was under enemy attack, but not once do we ever hear of Joseph planning revenge against those that hurt him. However, we do see "the fruits of righteousness" come from his soul. The end result of his fruit is God's divine faithfulness. The Lord makes his enemies his footstool.

There was a woman who attended Antioch Church years ago whose name was Nolene Hunley. She was the sweetest woman you would ever want to meet. When her husband passed away, the devil would often come to her with foolishness and evil attacks. The enemy would cloud her thinking and make her think that God took her spouse because he did not love her. She told our Bible study class one day how she dealt with it. She explained, "When I have those thoughts, I remind myself of all the things God has done for me just that day, and it heals me from the inside out!" You see, if you want to get the enemy off of your back, shift your thinking from fear and doubt to fruit and faith. It is then that you will recall just how wonderful the Lord has really been to you.

• • •

Public Praise for the God Who Delivered You

> … which are by Jesus Christ, unto the glory and praise of God.
>
> Phil. 1:11b

Enemy attacks are very real, but remember that God is a God of deliverance! There may be times when all seems lost, but God will take care of you. You see, during attacks of the enemy, some Christians stop worshipping the Lord and become unthankful. I submit that these moments of attack are the most crucial times to realize that God has done more for you than you could ever have imagined. He did this through Christ so that you would have something to give God glory and praise for. This is why you never cease to bless God during moments that the enemy is busy in your life. It is during these times that you should rejoice even more.

As this passage concludes, Paul gives us the basis for all that has taken place and our proper response to it. He declares that everything we have has come by Jesus Christ, and the reason the Lord has afforded it all is for the "glory and praise of God." How wonderful! Here's a man living on death row, attacked by the enemy, and talked about by other believers who are trying to do him harm. Yet he has the faith to say, "unto the glory and praise of God." Either Paul is losing his mind or he understands something that we need to grasp. Paul understands that there is power in blessing the Lord when dealing with enemy attacks. The good news is that if it was helpful for Paul in jail, it is helpful for you too.

I have always made the contention that the church should be a noisy place. The reason for this is that there are living testimonies sitting in every seat and monuments of mercy standing in every pair of shoes.

When God's people gather for worship, there are always people present who have seen the enemy attack their lives and know firsthand the goodness of God and his delivering power. When the testimony that is behind them comes from a thankful heart within them, it comes forth as praise unto God!

This is exactly what happened to Miriam in Exodus 15:20. When Miriam, sister of Moses, considered how the Lord had just delivered them from the hand of the enemy, she could not hold her peace. She reached for her tambourine and started to dance, celebrate, and worship the God that had blessed her. She publicly and intelligently worshiped the God that had delivered her people from bondage and oppression. In my heart, it is common sense. When God gives you strength at a time of weakness, when he gives you help when no one else is able, and when he grants you deliverance when the devil is trying to destroy you, praise is what he deserves!

My wife Dorrie and I have adopted two wonderful children. Sumone is four years old and Jonathan is two. As you can probably imagine, they have added a great deal of excitement to our lives. They keep us on our toes at all times. Lately, Jonathan has started to potty train. This is a totally new concept for me. Someone forgot to tell me that people do not just come out knowing how to properly make use of the facilities. My wife has been telling me how we should respond when Jonathan does well in this area. In fact, she tells me that we have to applaud him when he does everything the right way. So we have rules of praise in our house. When Jonathan does the right thing, at the right time, in the right place, we have to shout and cheer him on. The other day it hit me like a ton of bricks from heaven. If I could shout and applaud a two-year-old for doing the right thing, in the right place, at the right time, what about the God of the universe! In the midst of enemy attack and times of discomfort, God is still worthy of being honored, worshiped, and publicly praised.

It happened to Valarie Gibson. Her life was attacked and she did not know why, but she stood firmly on the word of God and prayer. Her family prayed, her friends prayed, and she stood on her convictions. It lasted two years! Can you imagine that? Two years of going to court. Two years of attorneys and fees. Two years of wondering. Two years of hoping. Two years of having her character attacked, and two years of trying to move forward while working under the thick fog of a federal indictment. But God came through for her and delivered her like only he could! In January 2007, she was completely vindicated of all of the charges against her. When asked how she felt, her reply was outstanding. She said, "When the enemy attacked, God delivered! He can be trusted!" Remember this: Just as God did it for Val, he will do it for you.

IT'S BEEN CRAZY, BUT I'M HANGING TOUGH

> But I would ye should understand, brethren, that the things which happened unto me have fallen out rather unto the furtherance of the gospel; So that my bonds in Christ are manifest in all the palace, and in all other places; And many of the brethren in the Lord, waxing confident by my bonds, are much more bold to speak the word without fear. Some indeed preach Christ even of envy and strife; and some also of good will: The one preach Christ of contention, not sincerely, supposing to add affliction to my bonds: But the other of love, knowing that I am set for the defense of the gospel. What then? notwithstanding, every way, whether in pretence, or in truth, Christ is preached; and I therein do rejoice, yea, and will rejoice.
>
> Phil. 1:12–18

Okay, I am guilty. I like being nosey. I try really hard to mind my own business, but when the news is worth listening to, I listen. Maybe it is not being nosey; maybe it is just eavesdropping. Whatever you call it, there are times when I am guilty of it and I just cannot help myself.

Not long ago, I stood near a group of men in a long line at Wal-Mart. Although I only had a few items and could have easily gone to the express line, I could not let their conversation go. So I did what you would have done; I stayed there and listened.

One of the men apparently had been through a season of good weather and blessings in his life. He boasted of how life had been for him. His children were off to college and things were going well. He was thinking about retiring from Exxon Mobil and things were as sweet as a tall glass of lemonade with just the right amount of sugar.

Another young man jumped into the dialogue, but all he did was complain about everything. He was married, but his wife was getting on his nerves. He had children, but they just weren't doing the right things. To make matters worse, he hated his job but had bills to pay.

Yet one of the men blessed me deeply. He said, "Well it's been crazy, but I'm hanging tough!" He explained, "I do not have a job right now, and things are tight. I was sick, and I missed quite a bit of work. When I ran out of sick time I stopped getting paid. My oldest son is really struggling, and I am trying to make ends meet. I went to get my meds the other day and one bottle of my pills cost nearly $900. But through it all, God has been good to me! My lights are on, my bills are paid, and I know it's going to be all right. It's been crazy for me, but I am hanging tough!"

Have you been at the point in life where your story sounds like his? Has it been to the point where you can say, "It's been crazy, but I'm hanging tough"? Here's the real deal: Life can be a serious trip. You can have some good days. You can have some rainy days. You can have some heart breaking days. And if you live long enough, you can have some crazy days!

A crazy day happens when you go to work and find yourself laid off; yet the bills keep on coming, and it seems like someone forgot to tell your lien holder that you can not give what you do not have. A crazy day is when you go to the doctor for a check-up and leave with a diagnosis that you do not understand, a prescription that you cannot pronounce, and a problem that only God can fix. A crazy day is when you find yourself choosing a casket for a loved-one you just knew would keep living, but they are now gone, and you are left to deal with it. Have you ever been there before? The truth is, life can throw some crazy days at you. But when it does, you have to get a grip on your faith in God and find the strength to say what the brother said in a Wal-Mart line not long ago: "It's been crazy for me, but I'm hanging tough!"

If there is anyone who fully understood what it was like to see life get crazy on them and still hang tough, it was the Apostle Paul. In fact, either Paul had lost his mind, or he knew something about God that all of us need to know in order to hang on when life gets tough. If you were to say, "Paul, Nero is talking about killing you as soon as he gets a chance." Paul would reply by saying, "That's okay; for to me to live is Christ and to die is gain" (Philippians 1:21). If you were to say, "Hey, Paul, you don't have much money and your resources are really running low." Paul would smile and declare, "Listen, I know how to be broke and I know how to have more than enough of what I need. But no matter what my case looks like, I am content because God takes care of me." And if you were to say, "Paul, aren't you worried about your future at all?" Paul would smile and say, "Do not worry about anything, but with prayer and supplication with thanksgiving let your prayerful requests be made known to the Lord and the peace of God shall surely keep your mind and soul through Christ. Rejoice in the Lord always and again I say, rejoice!" (Philippians 4:4).

What the great Apostle is really saying is this: "It's been crazy for me, but I'm hanging tough!" Now, here's the good news. If Paul could declare this, you can declare it too. If Paul could live it, you can live it. And if Paul could do it, you can do it! Things might be crazy, but it is not time to quit, give up, or throw in your towel. It is time for you to hang tough and not let go!

• • •

Remain Faithful In Your Witness

> But I would ye should understand, brethren, that the things which happened unto me have fallen out rather unto the furtherance of the gospel; So that my bonds in Christ are manifest in all the palace, and in all other places; And many of the brethren in the Lord, waxing confident by my bonds, are much more bold to speak the word without fear.
>
> Phil. 1:12–14

God has done some wonderful, amazing, and life-changing things for you, hasn't he? Let me pose a few good questions that should provoke a personal moment of reflection for you. Has the Lord ever opened a door for you that only he could open? Has God ever healed your body from an illness and given you your strength back? Has our wonderful Savior ever delivered you from something that could have been harmful for you if you had continued in it? Has our Master ever strengthened you in a time of weakness and turned a moment of midnight into day? Without a doubt, your story says that God has been there for you over, and over, and over again. The real truth of the matter is that you have a testimony to tell, and if no one else tells it, you should. Your story is your story. Share it!

Paul now moves to the section of the letter where he gives the Philippians the report on how things are going with him personally. Paul's report is awesome. In a nutshell, he tells the Philippian church,

"They have my hands locked, but my lips are loose! Every time I get a chance, I tell somebody else the good news. I open my mouth and let them know what he has done for me. In fact, there is a Roman guard locked to me. They are working in shifts. And every time one of them comes to lock himself to me, I take it as an opportunity to tell him about the grace of God!" Paul goes deeper by making it clear that his witnessing is actually helping others grow stronger in the faith and now they are sharing the gospel too.

Often when Christians hear the word "witnessing" surface or the idea of sharing the gospel with other people, they are quick to surmise that it is the job of the preacher. But nothing could be further from the truth. God has given you something that he did not give anyone else. He gave you your story. So even if you do not know the story of Moses and Joshua, or if you do not know the story of Abraham, Isaac, and Jacob, do not worry; just tell yours. The more you tell your story, the better you feel about you, your God, and your current condition.

Jeremiah put it best. He was a young prophet called by God to declare and share his word during a tough season of Israel's history. There were times when he did not want to share the news that God had given him. There were times when he wanted to just keep his mouth closed and say nothing, but every time he tried to keep quiet he experienced a phenomenon.

He felt like there was fire shut up in his bones (Jeremiah 20:9).

I was raised in a church where people could share their testimonies if they so desired. It was a part of the normal Sunday morning worship format. There was an old mother of the church that would never, ever let this opportunity pass her by. She told her story every Sunday morning; even if it was the same story that she told the last time she stood at the microphone. In total honesty, she told her story so often that we all knew it from memory, from start to finish. One day someone found the nerve to ask her why she had to testify every week. I will never forget her answer as long as I live. She explained, "Honey, I am a sickly woman. Many times when I come here I am not feeling too well at all. But the more I tell my story, the better I feel. I have to remind myself of what he has done for me and where he has brought me from. And the more I talk, the better I feel. If I don't share my story with y'all, I am going to tell somebody else just how good the Lord has been to me." Now, if telling her story made her feel better, what about you sharing yours? When things are tough, it's time to remind yourself just how great the Lord has been in your life by sharing your news with others.

• • •

Remain Fearless In Your Warfare

> Some indeed preach Christ even of envy and
> strife; and some also of good will: The one preach
> Christ of contention, not sincerely, supposing to
> add affliction to my bonds: But the other of love,
> knowing that I am set for the defence of the gospel.
>
> Phil. 1:15–17

Every real believer in the faith has enemies. However,
every enemy cannot hurt you. It's the ones that you let
get close to you that will hurt you the most. There's an
old cliché that holds true. It says, "Caesar had Brutus,
Jesus had Judas, and we have so-called-friends!" At
the end of the day, it is simply spiritual warfare at its
very best.

Paul had some enemies. In these verses he makes
it clear that there are some who are preaching Christ,
but they are doing it while also trying their best to hurt
him. He goes further by making the contention that
the people who are preaching against him are doing
so to hurt his ministry. There are numerous commentary writers who argue that there were those present
who stood against Paul because they disagreed with
his teachings. However, this would make the debate
and disagreement an issue of doctrine, and I beg to
differ. Here's why. The words "envy" and "strife" used
in verse fifteen are relational terms. Envy comes from
the heart of someone who wants to be who you are,
but cannot. Strife is a sin of the heart that is made

manifest with the mouth when people verbalize their feelings about you and try to make others feel the same way. With this in mind, there were those near Paul who were dangerous religious people who would say, "The gospel is good, but the preacher isn't worth much. We like what he says, but we don't like him." Paul clearly teaches us that while they were trying to hurt him, God was in the business of blessing him! The great news is that if this worked for Paul, it will also work for you.

One of the things that I have learned about the Lord is that he intentionally keeps believers in environments where they have enemies. There were times I wondered why a good God would do this. However, I figured it out with prayer and earnest observation. God gives us time in enemy territory because we are most productive in hostile environments. From those places come God's greatest blessings. He blesses us in the greatest way when we are behind enemy lines during seasons of spiritual battle.

One of my favorite Psalms is number twenty-three. I have had it memorized since I was a little boy. I have heard it read for various occasions, and have studied it in different settings and at different times. However, the other day while reading it for a morning devotional, I noticed something that I had never seen before. The psalmist says, "he prepareth a table before me in the presence of mine enemies." Wow, check God out! He prepares a table of blessing for

you, but look where he places it. It is not in the Car-
ribean under a nice coconut tree. It is not in Hawaii
at a sunny beach. God sets the table of your blessing
down in the presence of the enemy. It is here for two
reasons. First of all, it is in this place because God
wants you to know that you do not have to be afraid
of your enemy. Secondly, it is in this place because
there is still room at the table for anyone who wants
to become a part of the kingdom where our Lord rules
and reigns!

Not long ago I gained courage from a sister
who was having job trouble. Every week she would
go to work and it would be hell. I mean this literally. Demons would be on the loose, evil spirits often
lurked from every desk and meeting room. It was
hell. However, she did her job very well. When she
arrived at work she knew that she was walking into
enemy territory. When she told me what things were
like at work, I told her to find another job. She said,
"Pastor, God is on my side. And besides that, I am
not leaving because God is about to promote me. I
prayed about quitting and the Lord reminded me of
Joseph in Egypt. I am in my blessed place; it does not
look blessed but it is." Here's how the story unfolds.
A woman that she helped to get a job worked with
the coalition that tried to get her terminated. It created such a ruckus that the regional vice president and
district manager came to examine the incident. While
looking at her file, they said, "This is the type of per-

son we have been looking for! Where is she? We need you at the corporate headquarters." She got a new job, better pay, a corner office, and a secretary. Why? She was fearless in her warfare. She later smiled and told me, "It was a battle, but God was on my side. They meant it for bad, but God meant it for my good."

• • •

Remain Focused In Your Worship

What then? notwithstanding, every way, whether in pretence, or in truth, Christ is preached; and I therein do rejoice, yea, and will rejoice.

Phil. 1:18

God has not exempted us from the difficulties of life. What he has done is given every believer some tools to help us cope and conquer when we are under great duress. One of these wonderful tools is the blessing of joy. Joy is what we use that transforms tears and heartache into strength and blessing. No, everyday may not be an easy day. In fact, there will be some days and even some seasons where you just have to tie yourself a knot at the end of your rope, and just hang tough. While we are there, God has given us the tool of joy. It is what the Lord of Glory has blessed us with. Joy. I just love the way the word sounds. It is the springboard from which true worship comes forth.

Paul concludes by saying that it really does not

matter what they attempt to do to him as long as Jesus Christ is preached. He says, "I rejoice, yea and will rejoice!" The Greek term for rejoice here is *chairo*. It should be translated like this, "It has been crazy around here lately, but this joy that I have, people did not give it and cannot take it away." It means that no matter what happens to me, my personal celebration for what the Lord has done for me will not cease. The idea of joy runs through this letter like a red seam through a beautiful white dress. It is the theme of the entire letter. As Paul endures difficult circumstances, he has something that exists in his soul that will not let him give up, cease to preach, and get depressed. That *something* that the apostle has is joy.

Depression, anxiety, worry, and defeat need not be a permanent part of your life. But, grow to the point in grace where you too can echo the sentiment of the Apostle Paul where you say, "Rejoice and again I say, rejoice!" For the believer, rejoicing means to possess a spirit of worship and thanksgiving in the presence of circumstances that are anything but favorable. No, you should not be happy about having to endure moments of difficulty. But you should be thankful that God has given you the right to have joy while you endure it.

A few years ago I had the privilege of preaching a revival at a church in Silsbee, Texas. It is a small town just a few miles away from where I live. The church was filled with a rather spirited group of saints that really loved the preached word. While in the meeting, something extraordinary happened. One night while preaching, I noticed a woman who sat in the rear of the cathedral during the worship hour. I could not help but notice her, because every time I mentioned the name of Jesus she distracted me in a crazy way. Each time I mentioned the Lord's name she would take a stick and hit a tin can repeatedly. I know it sounds crazy, but this really happened. By the middle of my message she had worn my nerves thin. I was just about to ask someone to please stop her, but I am glad that I didn't. When the services ended I discovered that she could not talk due to a surgical procedure on her throat. So instead of sitting silently because she could not talk, she took a stick and beat a can. Now, that is real joy. That is remaining focused in your worship. That is being steadfast in your thanksgiving.

The line at Wal-Mart was long, and the young man asked the brother who said he was hanging tough an interesting question. He said rather sarcastically, "Hanging tough? What are you hanging on to?" And that's when the brother turned around and just started to testify. It was like having a revival at the register. In fact, that lane will never be the same again. The man who had been struggling, but was still thankful, said, "I am glad that you asked because you were complaining, and if I had your hand I would be even more grateful than I am right now. I am hanging not just to something, but somebody. He saved my soul from hell, he has been my friend when no one else bothered to care, he has given me strength when I was weak, he has given my life purpose when I did not think that life was worth living, and he has been and will remain the source of my joy. I am hanging onto the Lord! He is the one that makes me keep on keeping on every day of my life. Yeah, it's been crazy for me, but my friend, I'm still hanging tough!"

Here's the great news about the Lord—if a man with no job, limited resources, medical expenses that are out of reach, and a son that is losing his mind can hang tough, you can too. You just have to hold onto what he is holding onto, and that is Jesus Christ, Son of the living God. It may be crazy for you right now, but keep holding onto the Lord and hang tough!

I REFUSE TO LOSE

For I know that this shall turn to my salvation through your prayer, and the supply of the Spirit of Jesus Christ, According to my earnest expectation and my hope, that in nothing I shall be ashamed, but that with all boldness, as always, so now also Christ shall be magnified in my body, whether it be by life, or by death. For to me to live is Christ, and to die is gain. But if I live in the flesh, this is the fruit of my labour: yet what I shall choose I wot not. For I am in a strait betwixt two, having a desire to depart, and to be with Christ; which is far better: Nevertheless to abide in the flesh is more needful for you.

Phil. 1:19–24

I have been a sports enthusiast for many years; I love watching and playing sports. Not long ago I decided to follow a sport that I do not normally watch nor pay attention to—cycling. I watched the long grueling race called the Tour de France. I gained particular interest when repeated champion Lance Armstrong was accused of taking performance enhancing drugs to produce his repeated wins.

A reporter from a sports magazine posed this interesting question to Lance Armstrong during an interview: "Lance, did you do it? Did you use steroids or any form of performance-enhancing drugs to win?" Armstrong's answer blessed me. He replied, "No! I have never used performance-enhancing drugs. Instead of watching what goes into me they should keep their eyes on what's coming out of me." Candid and fearless, the reporter asked this world-renowned athlete, "How do you explain the numerous wins? How do you explain repeatedly beating the world's top athletes year after year?"

Armstrong responded in a fashion that helped me, and I hope that it helps you as you run this race of life. He said, "I show up the day of the race prepared to roll. I bring to the table an attitude that simply says losing is not an option!" Armstrong explained, "In spite of the opposition and the people that I am racing against, I tell myself one thing before I get there that sticks with me the entire race. It stays in my mind when I am tired and my legs are hurting. I think of it when it seems like it is impossible to continue on. I keep telling myself, 'I refuse to lose!'"

Posthumous professor and prelate, Dr. John C. Diamond, openly renounced being a part of the church because we are always losing. Diamond made the contention that we are losing our communities to addictions, even with churches on every corner. We are losing our men to prisons and penal systems. We are losing our morals to immorality. We are losing our minds and it appears that we are going crazy. We are losing our families to divorce. We are losing our children to BET! Diamond said, "I do not want to be a part of the church because all it does is lose!" Well, that may be true, but it is time for an adjustment to be made. We are on the Lord's side, which places every believer on the winning team.

As Paul writes in this portion of the verse, he offers some healing and hope to saints in a way that only the great apostle could do. He gets to a point where he argues that he will win no matter what happens. If he lives, he wins. He can continue preaching, teaching, and doing the work of the ministry. If he dies, he wins because in death he is with the Lord, and he knows that this is gain. The end result is awesome; he cannot lose in Christ! This certain victory in Christ causes an attitude that says I refuse to lose in this life or the life that is to come.

Have you arrived at the place in your faith journey with Jesus Christ where you can say, "I refuse to lose"? If you have, praise the Lord! You may need an attitude check if you haven't. Paul has an attitude of victory, and he has it from prison. Victory belongs to you in Christ, but you must have an attitude that says, "I refuse to lose." In this chapter we want to explore some of the attitudes that are apparent in this passage, so that we might gain a winning attitude and dwell in total victory as we run this Christian race for the Lord that we love.

. . .

The Attitude of Complete Deliverance

For I know that this shall turn to my salvation through your prayer, and the supply of the Spirit of Jesus Christ,

Phil. 1:19

There's a saying that comes from the words of an old hymn that holds true even today. Older saints used it quite a bit when they did not know how things were going to work out. Here's what they sang: "The Lord will make a way somehow!" This was simply a way of saying: "The Lord has brought me to where I am. I am trapped between a rock and a hard place, and I do not know how I am going to make it on my own now. Yet, having God with me, I am certain that everything is going to be all right. How? Because I know that the Lord will make a way somehow! "

Paul gives us the make-up of the "somehow" that leads to his complete deliverance and victory. He says, "I know ... your prayer, and the supply of the Spirit." In short, Paul says that it has been rough, but it's okay because God is going to deliver me. There is an interesting figure of speech here called a *metonymy*. Metonymy is the intermingling of one idea with another. Paul says it was your prayers, but it was also God's provisions that saw me through. The more I know and the more you pray, the more God supplies.

The word used to describe the supply is *epichorgia*. It is the same term used to describe the flowing waters of a river. River water flows all of the time like God's blessings and provisions in your life. It flows in every season; summer, winter, spring, and fall. It flows on good days and tough days. God keeps providing!

One great philosopher made the following observation about God: He is at his very best when you have arrived at a point where your hands are too small for the task, and you have to rely on his hands to be big enough to handle it all. It is then, and only then, that we see and encounter the majesty of God's divine provision.

One day there was a huge crowd of people near Jesus and they were hungry and tired, so a great idea arose. Let's feed them. However, there was a problem. There weren't enough resources. To put it plainly, they just didn't have enough food. But Jesus delivered. He not only fed them; they had leftovers. It is what I call divine elasticity. God will take what you have and stretch it beyond your wildest dreams or thoughts.

Rachel Alexander of Plaquemine, Louisiana, understands this idea of complete deliverance. She purchased a new home, and one week later her employer (the plant) shut an entire unit down. She was laid off without any notice at all. Her fourteen-year-old daughter asked her what they were going to do. She said, "Baby, my mother always said the Lord will make a way somehow." She told her church, and the people prayed. The river of God's divine provision just kept on flowing. When the light bill was due, the river flowed, and God paid the bill. When the mortgage was due, the river flowed, and God paid it! Her daughter asked her how it could be. Rachel replied with confidence, "If you trust him and never doubt he will see you through." Have you ever seen his river flow in your life? God will provide!

• • •

The Attitude of Confident Discovery

> According to my earnest expectation and my hope, that in nothing I shall be ashamed, but that with all boldness, as always, so now also Christ shall be magnified in my body, whether it be by life, or by death.
>
> Phil. 1:20

I have learned how to live the Christian life with a degree of expectancy. I know that God is able, and I live expecting God to do things for me that no one else could ever do. I walk with God expecting him to do supernatural things. Expectancy is the spiritual attitude that I live with each day. I have learned that if you expect nothing, you often get nothing. Conversely, when you expect great things from a great God, he does great things for you.

This is the attitude of the Apostle Paul in Philippi.

In fact, he says, "my earnest expectation." This phrase is a tongue twister in the Greek language. It comes from the word *apokatadokia*. Apokatadokia is a trilogy of words that make up one word. *Apo* means to lift the head. *Kata* means to stretch the neck. Lastly, *dokia* means to strain the eye. Thus, great expectation means to lift the head, stretch the neck, and strain the eye. This is the position that you should be in when looking for God to move in your life. You should also be ready to magnify the Lord in your body when you do it. The word magnify is *megaluna*. *Mega* means large and *luna* has solar overtones. It means to make that which is distant closer. The idea is that when expectancy becomes a reality, God gets glory that comes from the place that he has blessed.

Too many of us spend time inspecting what God says instead of expecting what God has promised. A centurion who had a servant at home near death approached Jesus with his problem one day. He told Jesus of his servants' condition. It was then that the centurion demonstrated his attitude of expectation, and said, "You do not have to come to my house. Just speak the word!" (Matthew 8:5–11, KJV). The centurion was not busy inspecting what the Lord said. Instead of inspecting what was said, he was living in the hope and expectation of what the Lord had promised … and the rest is history.

My mother used to drop me off at grade school in Houston, Texas. Each day I would kindly remind her that the school session ended at 3:15 p.m. However, it never failed; I would be the last student picked up and I would just have to wait on her arrival. After a while, all of the cars looked alike. As I sat there waiting on her, I would stretch my neck, strain my eyes, and keep my headed lifted. I would be waiting in expectancy for her arrival. By the time she would get there, I would be ready for her arrival and rejoicing in my heart. This is how believers should be with the promises of God. This is the attitude that is reflected in the passage. It is an attitude that says God is going to come through, and I am expecting it!

• • •

The Attitude of Christ-Centered Determination

> For to me to live is Christ, and to die is gain. But if I live in the flesh, this is the fruit of my labour: yet what I shall choose I wot not. For I am in a strait betwixt two, having a desire to depart, and to be with Christ; which is far better: Nevertheless to abide in the flesh is more needful for you.
>
> Phil. 1:21–24

The enemy wants you to quit. He wants you to give up. He wants you to lose. He wants you to worry about things you cannot control, lose sight of things that are real, forget about God's goodness, and lose. If you are going to win in life you have to be determined to do it.

Paul says: "For to me to live is Christ and to die is gain" (Philippians 1:21). This passage exudes his total determination. Paul says I am going to win no matter what. If I live, I win; Jesus is with me and I can help you in the faith. If I die, I win because I've always desired to be near the Lord and done with all of this. I am determined to win!

True determination comes when you are too stubborn to quit, too crazy to become discouraged, and too confident to consider losing as an option. There is a woman in the scriptures who had every reason to quit. Her story is found in the Gospel according to Mark, chapter five. She had been ill and suffering with bleeding and hemorrhaging for twelve long years. You may know her as "the woman with the issue of blood." She could have easily quit. Her story says that she spent all of her money on doctors, and instead of getting better, she got worse. She was seen as an unclean part of the community in which she lived. Thus, she was ostracized, criticized, and dehumanized. Yet she was determined. She pressed her way through the crowd and touched the hem of the garment of the Lord; she was healed instantly.

I was watching the Discovery Channel the other night when they started to show these beautiful pictures. They were gorgeous portraits, simply breathtaking. It came time for a commercial break and they announced that we would "meet the artist" when they returned. I started to change the channel, but I couldn't. To my surprise, the artist was not Van Gogh. It was not Picasso. It was a sixteen-year-old kid from the Midwest whose name was Robert Bilnosky. What's deep is that Bilnosky was born without arms and hands. The only way for him to paint was to learn to do it with his feet. Yes, that's right, with his feet. When the interviewer asked young Bilnosky how he did it, he told her it was painful. "I wanted to quit several times, but the more I did it, the more determined I was to do it! I am pretty good at it now." He added, "Isn't that why you came to see me? I'm pretty good right?" If Bilnosky could be determined enough to learn to paint with his feet and work through his pain, shouldn't you? Winning only comes through the attitude of a person that says, "I am determined!"

I really enjoyed the article about Lance Armstrong. As I read it, there were parts of it that overwhelmed me with joy. The reporter asked him how he could possibly account for all of his wins without steroid usage. It was then that Lance gave them the answer that I honestly feel was the root of all of his victories. Armstrong declared that the reason he won so many races was because he specialized in winning from behind. You see, unlike his competitors he does his best riding in the hill country, when others are too weak to continue to make the climb. It is then that he gives himself a pep talk and says, "I refuse to lose!"

I'M COMING OUT OF THIS!

And having this confidence, I know that I shall abide and continue with you all for your further-ance and joy in the faith; That your rejoicing may be more abundant in Jesus Christ for me by my coming to you again.

Phil. 1:25–26

Years ago, I left the church a very frustrated young man. My personal discontentment with the church was not without reason. Until that time I had always lived with the woeful misconception that church peo-ple were perfect and had only then begun to realize that was not the case. First of all, the preacher was flawed. I have the liberty of saying that because he was my father. Everyone else saw the perfect pastor; yet I also saw the not-so-perfect man. The soloist in the choir was sinful, and people always commented that he was "sweet." I came to discover later that what they coined as sweet was really gay. The men serving as deacons would count money during worship, and if they finished early enough they would step outside, stand under a tree, have a smoke, and discuss the aesthetic beauty of the feminine creatures parked in the pews. To hurt me even deeper, I was informed through the church grapevine that some of the people who I really looked up to (i.e. mission sisters and mothers of the church) had backgrounds that would make sinful mini-skirt wearing sisters look like nuns. As though that were not enough, the members of the church were no more righteous than the rest. They merely sat quietly and listened for gossip so that they could throw rocks at people and then hide their hands. Of course none of them were without fault, and we all know that people in glass houses should not throw stones.

So, in my frustration, I left the church. I made a decision that if I was going to hell, I might as well do it first class! I mean, why kid around with it, right? As far as I was concerned, people in church were only learning the Bible to become smart sinners and not serious saints. However, by the time I was in my mid-twenties something extraordinary happened to me that I will never forget. I grew up. Yes, I matured, and I started to realize that the church of God was not a place where perfect people gathered each week. On the contrary, church is a place for struggling people who are constantly coming out of issues that the enemy is trying to bind them with.

My study of scripture has taught me that there are demons dispatched from hell's core whose very purpose is to keep God's people in spiritual shackles. The shackles are to ensure that the people Jesus died for never experience true liberation, because if we did we would turn the world upside down and then right side up for the cause of Christ! I read a book a few years ago, where a local pastor realized that many of his members were struggling with spiritual freedom in Jesus Christ. In response, he started to set up private prayer sessions with each of them that he called "freedom appointments." These appointments were designed for people who were bound to come in and encounter the Holy Ghost, the truth of scripture, the love of Jesus Christ, and leave liberated.

In many instances the pastor interviewed people who had been bound and tied by demonic forces and wanted to be free. One woman had been bruised deeply in her past and struggled with issues of forgiveness. Another he interviewed struggled with issues of pornography. Another grappled with issues of belief in voodoo and witchcraft. But the one that blew my mind was the story of the lady whose name was Mabel. Mabel showed up for her personal freedom appointment, and when he asked her if she was ready to be set free, her answer blessed me from just reading it. She said, and I quote, "I would not be here if I weren't. I have struggled with this demon all of my life and I want you to know that today is my day. I am coming out of this!"

I rejoiced and shouted when I read her expression.

"I'm coming out of this!" What a concept. Here's the truth, and take it for what it is worth to you, all of us have some things that we need freedom appointments for. For some, it is jealousy. For others, the issue is anger, and still for others it is some type of moral collapse. Why live bound when Jesus died to set us free? Declare it with your tongue, believe it in your heart, live it by faith, and receive it in your spirit: "I'm coming out of this!" For some it is addictive gambling. For others it is excessive spending. Some struggle with depression, thoughts of suicide, and ideas of quitting when God is just getting started. Say this aloud as you read this chapter, "I'm coming out of this!"

In fact, consider this chapter your personal freedom appointment. God is going to take his word and heal you with it. Now is the time to declare liberty, peace, healing and deliverance! Today is the day that your life takes a turn for the better. It is the day that your life gains a blessing that even the enemy cannot steal. Today is the day that God moves on the altar of your heart so that strength and blessing are the end result. Here is where it all starts. With God's healing help, you can declare in faith the core thought of this text, "I'm coming out of this!"

In the passage, Paul is locked up in prison. He has given us the report that some are trying to hurt him, but the more they try, the more God blesses him. He tells the church that he is caught between two ideas. He wants to go home and be with the Lord and he desires to stay around and continue sharing the gospel message. It is in this verse that he makes a decision that comes from the heart of the Lord!

In layman's terms, what Paul says is, "Yes, I'm on lock down right now. I am under house arrest, but my current condition does not dictate or define my future position. I do not care about Nero. I do not care about the Praetorian Guard or the number of haters trying to hurt me. I am locked up, but I am confident of this thing: "I know that I shall abide and continue with you all for your furtherance and joy in the faith; that your rejoicing may be more abundant in Jesus Christ for me by my coming to you again" (Philippians 1:25–26).

Can you feel his passion? He is locked up, but he says, "I am coming to you again!" His head is on the chopping block, and things look grim, yet he says, "I am coming to you again!" Okay, let me give you a retranslation of this verse my way. The great apostle is declaring, "Where I am now is not where I am going to end up. I have issues with bondage right now, but trust me, I'm coming out of this!"

By taking on the passion of Paul, you too can declare victory over your issues. Speak to God earnestly and say, "Yes Lord, I love you, but I have some issues I need your help with." Profess with your mouth as you read this passage, "I'm coming out of this!" Say in faith, "I will no longer be bound by the circumstances of life. I'm coming out of this!"

Through faithful declaration, the couple whose

marriage is on the rocks and considering divorce as an option can gain strength. For the person who tithes and gives but struggles financially every week, I assure you that your harvest is going to come in. There is liberation for the believer who worries too much, freedom for the saint who is constantly filled with anxiety and stress, and emancipation to the new convert who is still trapped in some private sins that they need to come out of. Declare it with your mouth and speak in total belief, "I'm coming out of this!"

There are several ways to be freed from the enemy's shackles and find healing, wholeness, freedom, and strength in Jesus Christ. From just two verses of Paul's teachings, there are several principles that we can gain from, and if practiced, they will surely help you not just say but live the words that you have been declaring.

• • •

Be Confident in the Faith

And having this confidence...

Phil. 1:25a

It was a scene that I will never forget. I went to a hospice facility to visit a dying mother of a very dear friend. While sharing with them, I was asked to pray with several other families who had ill loved ones there. As I went from room to room praying for people, it became evident which rooms had believers in them. In one room lay a man whose family was yelling and screaming. They were fighting amongst themselves and bickering. But in the room just across the hall there was a young man who had died just moments before. The atmosphere was filled with a spirit of joy (not happiness). His family was sad to see him leave, but glad to see his pain cease. He was only fourteen years old. Tears rolled down their cheeks, and I watched his mother stroke his head and sing a hymn. Yes, that's right, she sung a hymn. Can you see this in your mind? Her son just passed and she is worshipping God with a song. It was a song that I had not heard in quite some time. The lyrics spoke, "'Tis so sweet just to trust in Jesus; just to take him at his word." Now let me ask you, was the family of this fourteen-year-old kid crazy? Were they losing it? Were they suffering from some form of personal denial regarding the death of this child? No, they were confident. They were confident that God was too good to be bad, too perfect to make a mistake, and too gracious to be mean.

Let's stop and consider some questions on a very personal level. Has God ever let you down before? Has the Lord ever turned his back on you for your ruin or hurt? Has he ever sought to hurt you for the purpose of your demise and ruin? Here's the true answer: no! The best news of the day is that he has never failed you. Your testimony with God says that he is able.

When things have been shaky in your life, he has been a rock that keeps you stable. Your story says that in spite of sickness, pain, and moments of serious difficulty, God has been good. When people that you thought you could depend on walked out of your life, you discovered that God was ever present and faithful. He has never failed you and because of that you can be confident in him

The Apostle Paul says, "And having this confidence. " The word choice here is so rich. It is the term *pi-tho*. It means to be totally convinced. It means to know without a doubt, to be settled on the issue. Even more so, what's deep is that the same term is used of two soldiers who have each other's back in a time of battle. It means to trust because it has been proven and tested and found trustworthy. In those few words, Paul gives us shouting news. He says unambiguously that by now you should be confident that God can do it because you have had to fight tough battles with him on your side before, and he has proven to be a champion on the battlefield of your human existence. He is reminding you that in every one of the battles you have fought, the Lord had your back, front, sides, head, and feet all covered!

It is easy to lose confidence in human kind. People tend to change like the weather. It is easy to lose confidence in systems. They are made and designed by people that are flawed. It is easy to lose confidence in surgeons and scientists. They are human and they often make mistakes. It is easy to lose confidence in money. There are some things that it will never buy. It is easy to lose confidence in knowledge. There are always things that we do not know. But it is hard to lose confidence in God. For God knows all, sees all, controls all, possesses all, and is always there.

Did you know that healing and deliverance happens when saints have confidence in Jesus? Let me show you what I mean. In John 11, Lazarus is dead. In fact, he is so dead that rigor mortis has come and gone and his body had already begun to carry an odor. Then Jesus shows up. Mary has an attitude. She is not running out to meet him because she called him four days ago and he did not come. Still, Martha runs out to meet him. She initially says to him that if he had been there her brother would not have died. Paraphrased simply, Jesus responds by saying, "Girl, do not lose your confidence. Do not forget who I am! I am the resurrection and the life." Jesus then asks Martha a very important question. He asks her, "Do you believe that I can do it?" and her answer is yes! They get to the grave and when Jesus calls Lazarus' name, he comes out! Lazarus comes out, not just because Jesus called him, but because there was someone nearby who had confidence that Jesus could bring him out.

Every year I am blessed to share in the Lilly Grove Baptist Church's Men's Day Celebration. During one year's celebration, a brother gave me his twenty-year sobriety chip. Twenty years of liberty.

Twenty years of freedom from drug addiction. Twenty years! When I asked him what keeps him, he said quite simply, "I am powerless, but I am confident in the hands of God. It's been twenty years and he has never let me down." Can you hear the healing in that? If you are going to come out of it you must be confident that God is an able God.

• • •

Be Convinced in the Heart and Verbal with the Mouth

... I know that I shall abide and continue with you
all for your furtherance and joy of faith

Phil. 1:25b

If you really want to see God move mightily in your life, you are going to have to change the way you talk. You will never speak defeat and experience victory. You will never speak sickness and encounter healing. In short, what you say is what you will see. All too often, I hear people who are poor say things like, "I am tired of being broke." I hear people who have been ill tell others how sick they are. Stop saying that! I learned years ago from my mother, that if you do not have anything good to say, do not say anything at all. If you are sick and you just have to talk about it, tell people that you are in the process of being healed, and the Lord is just taking his time with you. If you are struggling financially, tell people that you are in a season of testing, but your season of blessing is right around the corner. Your healing and deliverance are on the tip of your tongue!

In this passage, Paul has a secret that he lets us in on. It is the secret to his deliverance. Paul declares, "I know that I shall abide and continue with you all for your furtherance and joy of faith." The words "know" and "abide" leap out of the passage and grab me like a bass hooked on a lure. The word "know" comes from the Greek term *gnosko.* Paul is fond of this term and uses it often in his writings. It means to know by way of personal encounter or to know because of what has been experienced. "Abide" comes from the term *meno,* which means to stay. The term was used to describe a rock after a windstorm had blown. The sand may have moved, but the rock is still present. When these two terms are put together in the text, Paul's secret is evident. He has no doubt that he is not leaving until the Lord says otherwise.

However, the awesome part about this sentence construct is not found in the Greek, but in the English grammar. Paul says, "I know that I am not going anywhere until the Lord calls me." He proclaims, "I am not going anywhere; I am staying here until the Lord says otherwise and I do not care who likes it or not!" In short, he believes it enough to declare it. And because he has declared with his mouth, he lives it in the faith.

Here is the core principle to liberation. There will never be real emancipation without steadfast declaration. If you are going to possess it, you must first proclaim it. Now, this is not a name it and claim it deal. However, it is a matter of heart and head harmony. What the mouth speaks the heart must believe.

The Bible speaks to us concerning this very issue. "Death and life are in the power of the tongue" (Proverbs 18:21a). This concept is so awesome. You do not get what you see, but you gain what you say. Jesus Christ taught this very same potent concept when he told his disciples that in order to move a mountain they would have to speak to it (Matthew 17:20, KJV).

Doctors told Michelle Manning that she would never walk again, but she refused to accept that report. Every day, she told herself that she was going to walk. Her doctor told her that as soon as she accepted the fact that she could not walk, the faster she would be able to adjust and move on. Michelle told him she had accepted what was said, it just came from another doctor. Retranslated: "I heard what you said, but I'm coming out of this!" Michelle prayed and went through therapy every day, and the nerve endings in her back miraculously started to repair themselves. The doctors were amazed and used her body as a case study. The end result was Michelle up and walking, and doctors did not know how it happened. Doctors repeatedly asked her about her restoration, and she told them bluntly, "My healing is spiritual. I heard what you said, but I only accepted and believed what the Lord said." Michelle told her neurologists that she would routinely hold a Bible and declare it over her life and body, and the rest is history. Now, if she is walking because of what she believed and declared, you can be sure that what you believe and declare will do the same. If you are going to come out of this, believe it with your heart and speak it with your mouth.

* * *

Be Constant In Your Rejoicing

That your rejoicing may be more abundant in Jesus Christ for me by my coming to you again.

Phil. 1:26

I was raised with a mother that would not let children drink coffee. So, when I would go and stay with Big Mama, my mother's mother, I would beg her for coffee. Big Mama would remind me that my mother did not want me to have a cup of coffee, but she would always follow that by saying, "Let me see what Big Mama can do for you." It was then that she would get to work. She would fill her cup to the brim, pour in her cream, and add two spoonfuls of sugar; and the coffee would run over into her saucer. Big Mama would keep the cup, give me the saucer, and utter with a smile, "Your Mama said you could not have a cup, but she did not say you couldn't have a saucer. It's not a cup, honey, but it is just as good."

I am reminded of this because this is how rejoicing for the Christian should be. You should have so much joy it should just run over. This is a key element in being healed and delivered. The trick of the enemy is to get you to look at what you don't have instead of being thankful for what you do have. The enemy often causes us to look at what God took, instead of being filled with a sense of gratitude for what he has left. If you want to see deliverance come into your life, I dare you to focus only on what you have and be thankful for it. Rejoicing brings about healing and freedom.

In the verse, Paul states, "That your rejoicing may be more abundant." The word rejoicing is *kow-ka-mah*. It refers to the outward expression of a saint that is a reflection of their inward joy. In short, it means to express joy with the lips. It means to boast and give glory with the mouth. The term "abundant" means to overflow. It means to run over the side. It suggests the idea of having more than enough. Paul says to this faithful church, "Hold on to your joy until I arrive, that way the celebration will be in full bloom when I show up."

I have an argument regarding real rejoicing. I honestly believe that rejoicing is not real rejoicing until it does at least two things: it should bless God and better others. If your joy does not give glory to God, it is not real joy. If your rejoicing does not strengthen someone else in the journey, you don't have much. Conversely, when your rejoicing causes others to gain strength and

God to be honored with glory, then your rejoicing is for real! When was the last time your rejoicing made someone else better? When was the last time that your joy put a smile on the face of Jesus Christ? That alone is real joy.

A beautiful portrait of this kind of rejoicing is seen in Acts 16:16. Paul and Silas are in jail in Philippi. Things are not going well for them at all. They have been arrested on false charges and beaten terribly. They are in a dungeon, but they do not let where they are define where they are headed. In the midst of a crisis, they start to rejoice. Their cup gets so full that it overflows, and others are saved because of who they have living inside of them. The earth quaked, the captives went free, and the lost were saved. It all happened when their rejoicing became real before God.

Kimberly Jones, alias Lil' Kim, was recently released from a federal penal facility where she spent nearly a year in jail for charges of perjury. I could not help but notice that before she got out they started having prerelease celebrations. In fact, four months before her release, they were printing T-shirts. One young lady said, "We love Kim and we want to celebrate her getting out." I said to myself, "Wow, a coming out party." What an idea. What a concept. I know that Christians in the church have to be careful about what we borrow from secular sources, but this is one that I like. Parties to celebrate your release before you come out. What if the church borrowed that concept and started to have prerelease celebrations? We could call them our "I'm coming out of this!" celebration." Can you just imagine what worship would look like? If God is faithful to his word, and he is, we can celebrate our release from bondage with a premeditated thank you for the healing that is yet to come. For even now, he alone is worthy to be praised!

Yes, I left church years ago because none of the people were righteous. However, it was when I returned that I ran into my biggest discovery of all; I was not flawless either! I was so busy judging others that I did not take any time to judge myself. When I looked closely at myself I realized that what I needed was a Savior and a God. I needed someone bigger than me who could save me from my sin and heal me from within. Oh, I came back to church all right, but I returned with a new attitude. I came back with an attitude that said, "I'm coming out of this!" I returned with an attitude that said, "Jesus died and rose for me to have it, and I refuse to leave the house of God without it. I want the salvation that he offers, the healing that he grants, the direction that he gives, the discipline that he bestows, and the harvest that is promised!"

I did not understand that the church was for people who were in the midst of the struggle and who were coming out of things that the enemy had tried to ensnare them with. So, I watched my own behavior, and instead of judging them, I started shouting with them. The more I worshipped, the better I felt. When they would have an altar call, I would love to hear the words to the old hymn "Amazing Grace." It has become the anthem of my soul. God is a God who heals and delivers. His grace sets us free. If you desire the freedom that only he can give, stand firmly in the faith, declare with your mouth, and believe in your heart the message that says in faith, "I'm coming out of this!"

PREPARE TO DO BATTLE!

Only let your conversation be as it becometh the gospel of Christ: that whether I come and see you, or else be absent, I may hear of your affairs, that ye stand fast in one spirit, with one mind striving together for the faith of the gospel; And in nothing terrified by your adversaries: which is to them an evident token of perdition, but to you of salvation, and that of God. For unto you it is given in the behalf of Christ, not only to believe on him, but also to suffer for his sake; Having the same conflict which ye saw in me, and now hear to be in me.

Phil. 1:27–30

For years I have been a movie buff. I love the big screen. Nothing relaxes me more than to sit down with a hot bag of popcorn and watch the action unfold. Action, adventure, and excitement just give me a thrill. Yes, I also like an occasional love story, but too much of that and I find myself drifting off to sleep. For me, the movie of the year was entitled 300.

I know it is not the caliber of movie like a *Driving Ms. Daisy* or *The Color Purple,* but I love it!

The movie depicts scenes from the ancient Greek battle Thermopylae that took place in 480 BC. I had read about the battle as an undergrad and found it boring. In total honesty, I hated reading it. But I wanted to pass English composition, so I had no choice in the matter. For me, to read a work like that was about as painful as pulling teeth without Novocain. To the best of my recollection, I bought the Cliff Notes for this military saga and made a *C* in the course. I know it was not an *A,* but thank God I made it somehow.

Anyway, the battle had the powerful, ripped, and skilled men of Sparta against the great army of the Persian Empire. The Spartan army was under the leadership of Leonidas I, and they were badly outnumbered with the odds stacked against them. Despite this, they were well trained and prepared for battle. Their spears and swords were sharp, their shields were made of cast iron, the soldiers knew how to fight in hand-to-hand combat, and they were fearless. The Persian army was so vast that it would literally drink rivers dry. When they marched under the leadership of Xerxes I, the ground would shake, and the earth would quake. The Spartans were supposed to be doomed from the start. Astonishingly, for three days that small cluster of three hundred men from Sparta withstood eighty thousand men from one of the most powerful armies in the known world. They were able to do it, because when they made their way to the fight, they were prepared to do battle.

I love the movie. It gives me a rush, because when I watch the film I see a great parallel between their fight on the battlefield and our fight in the faith as believers in Jesus Christ. The only way for us to stand firm is to do what the Spartans did. We must show up each day prepared for battle.

There are many Christians who live defeated, dejected, and depressing lives, because they attempt to be good Christians without any time given to preparation. Consequently, when they get to the battlefield, they lose. They lose their last nerve and end up in anger. They lose their joy and end up in worry. They lose their focus and end up in total fear. Then there are others who spend time in prayer as they start each day's journey, they spend time in the word to hear the voice of God, and time in worship knowing that though the battle is on, they are warriors in the faith prepared for battle!

When we read the closing verses of Paul's letter, he is in the thick of battle, but like a strong warrior for Jesus Christ, he is prepared for the fight. He uses military terms to speak to the church of God. He says: "stand fast," "striving together," "in nothing being terrified of your adversaries," and "suffer for his sake." This aged apostle realizes that his group may be well outnumbered, but numbers are not everything. Paul knows that there may not be many Christians in the city, but there is a great deal of Christ in their hearts. The believers are often criticized, dehumanized, and rejected. In spite of these things, they are standing strong for the sake of the gospel of Jesus Christ.

The believer that thinks that they can live the Christian life without battle is like a running back who thinks he can run touchdowns without ever getting hit. In short, it is not going to happen. In this Christian campaign from earth to heaven, there will be some days when the battlefield is your living room, and you find yourself fighting for your family. There are other times when you will find yourself fighting as a missionary in a foreign country that is not embracing you, your culture, or the gospel you say you have to preach. And still, there will be other times you will have to fight just to keep your sanity. Whatever the case, the key to winning is to be on the Lord's side; be fearless in the faith and know that you will only stand victorious if you stand prepared for battle!

In this chapter, we will explore some of the strategies that prepared the Philippians to do battle. If it prepared them, it will also prepare you.

• • •

Focus On Your Conduct

Only let your conversation be as it becometh the gospel of Christ.

Phil. 1:27a

As I drove down Highway 105 one afternoon, I read a church billboard that made me turn around in the middle of the street and read it one more time. The sign read: "My greatest enemy is in-a-me." Sometimes my greatest enemy is within me. My real fight is that I know what's right. However, there are times that I just don't do what is right. I know better, but there are times when I don't do better. Thus, my fight is not always external; sometimes it is internal. There are times when I worry, and I need to trust. There are moments when I hold a grudge, when I need to forgive. There are seasons when I am in fear, and I should be in complete faith. Have you ever been at this place in your life?

In verse twenty-seven, Paul teaches us how to be prepared for battle when he says, "Let your conversation be as it becometh the gospel." The wording here is a bit confusing. Allow me to explain. The word "conversation" in our world means to talk or to communicate. But in Paul's time it meant to walk. In our culture, conversation refers to that which flows from your lips. In Paul's day it was that which came from your lifestyle. It is the word *politeo*. We borrow our word politics from it, and it should be translated as the word "citizenship." Paul says to make sure that your lifestyle "becometh" the gospel. The word "becometh" is really rich in meaning; it comes from the Greek word *axios*. We borrow our term axiom from it. Now, I did not learn every lesson taught in school, but I did learn that an axiom is that which is concrete and absolute in the English language. In algebra, an axiom means to put in a scale knowing that both parts are equal. (For example: 4 + 1 and 3 + 2 are equal. That is to say, when added they both equal five.)

In a nutshell, Paul says that if you are going to be prepared for battle and victorious in the faith, you are going to have to work on yourself to the point that your inward faith is seen in your outward walk. Thus, inward faith and outward walk are equal. You must live in such a way that what you believe guides how you behave. You must get to the point where the doctrines that you know, impact the deeds that you do. Paul says that your lifestyle should look like good news! And if that is not the case, you have some preparing to do.

You will never win great external battles until you first win some internal wars. Look at the life of Jesus Christ. According to Matthew 4, Jesus went into the wilderness and fasted for forty days and forty nights. Why? He needed to win some private battles before he started to win public wars. Jesus does this because he knows that if he could not win in private, he would lose in public. Now, if Jesus had to win first in private, what about every other Christian in the whole wide world?

I once met a married couple who were really struggling and on the verge of divorce. They were devout Christians, and yet they were having a really difficult time. The young lady reached a point where she resented her husband and everything that he stood for. During my time of sharing with them, I discovered that the problem with the young lady was not her husband; it was her father. She was thirty-one years old, and hated her father for things that he did and said to her when she was a child. She thought that if he was out of sight that he would be out of mind, but nothing could have been farther from the truth. She asked me what could be done to help her with this problem. I told her that she would never conquer what she refused to confront. My advice was simple, confront the inner demons with the power of Christ, and accept the healing that only Jesus can provide. She did it! She conquered what was happening on the inside, and it manifested on the outside in her marriage being healed. God healed their marriage by restoring her soul and getting her to deal with private issues that led to public victory. If this worked for them, it will work for you.

· · ·

Fight with Other Christians

… that whether I come and see you, or else be absent, I may hear of your affairs, that ye stand fast in one spirit, with one mind striving together for the faith of the gospel.

Phil. 1:27b

Sylvester Stallone is the Hollywood hunk known for his appearances in the movie *Rambo*. It's the kind of film that I like, but there is just one problem with it. Rambo is a one-man army that is able to take on all of his adversaries alone. It is a great film, yet totally unrealistic. In the Christian walk, there are no spiritual "Rambos." There is not one saint who can win every battle alone. Everybody needs somebody to fight with them. That's why you need the church. I know, you are saying that there are some messy people in the church. You are right, but I think we would agree that there are also some messy people in the mall, and that has not stopped you from shopping. The truth is, you need to be in the company of some people who are in the fight just like you are. Nevertheless, you do not want to fight with just anybody. You want to fight with some folks that know how to do spiritual combat.

Paul makes the contention that when you go to fight, do not go by yourself. Here is how he says it: "stand fast in one spirit, with one mind striving together for the faith." If you cannot do anything else, take a stand. Stand in a spirit of unity and oneness with other saints who are real. The term "striving together" comes from the Greek term *soon-atheleo.* "Soon" means *with* and "atheleo" is the term *athlete.* In combination, the terms refer to those who wear your colors and are on your team. Paul offers a word of caution not to fight by yourself but stay with your team. The tense, voice, and mood of the term means that it is interdependent. Interdependent simply means: I cannot win without you winning with me.

I have learned from years of living that you should not be concerned with who is fighting against you.

Instead it is who is fighting on your side that counts. If you have the right God on your side, trust me, everything is going to be all right. There is only one God that I know of who will walk with you into battle, help you in the midst of the fight, and remain with you until the battle is over. He is Jesus Christ, Son of the living God.

Picture this: Elisha is on a mountain and the Syrian army is about to attack. There is a young man there who is not skilled in battle and panics. Elisha says to the Lord, "Let's let him in on the real deal so that he can understand that we are not alone here." All of a sudden, the young man could see. His eyes were opened, and he could see chariots of fire all around him. He now feels confident that the army he is looking at will not overtake him. He knows that the army of the Lord is on his side.

My friend Jo-Jo had a twenty-inch huffy bicycle with nice reflectors and mirrors on it when we were about twelve years old. However, the day came when some guys from another neighborhood thought that they would look better riding it, so they took it from him at the corner store. All of the kids from our block tried to advise Jo-Jo that he should not go and try to get his bike alone. Still, in anger, rage, fury, and youthful ignorance, he tried it. Needless to say, the bruises, scars, and scratches taught him some valuable lessons. You see, we had some friends that you would want to do battle with, but Jo-Jo tried to do it by himself. He had access to some tough kids that knew how to fight, like Jock, Buffalo, Glue, and Nathan. They were the guys that you wanted fighting on your side, but Jo-Jo went alone. He came back limping and wounded. The next day he came to his senses, and Jo-Jo got prepared for battle. He rallied the troops, and we went together. When they saw us coming up the block, those guys who took my friend's bike kindly placed it out front for us to pick up and carry home. That's how it is with God! The enemy will take your stuff, and if you seek to fight alone, you will end up defeated. On the other hand, if you take your elder brother, Jesus, with you, along with a group of saints seasoned in spiritual battle, when the enemy gets a glimpse of who is with you he will sit your stuff out front. Why? Because we never fight alone; we fight with the Lord and other saints on our side.

. . .

Fearless in Chaos

And in nothing terrified by your adversaries: which is to them an evident token of perdition, but to you of salvation, and that of God.

Phil. 1:28

It was the fight of the century that put James "Buster" Douglass against "Iron" Mike Tyson for the heavy-weight championship of the world. I remember it clearly. Douglass was a forty-two to one underdog. In short, he was supposed to lose. Evidently someone forgot to tell him that. In the tenth round, James Douglass rocked the world by defeating one of the most feared boxers in the known world. As Tyson made his way to the locker room, the media interviewed the new heavyweight champion. When asked what his fight plan was, he said with passion and simplicity, "I was not afraid of him!" You see, it was a fight of fights, but Douglass won because he stood toe-to-toe with "Iron Mike" and was fearless in the ring.

Real saints possess a spiritual toughness that says, "Bring it on!" Paul shares this fearless nature with the Christians that are at Philippi. Here is what he says to them: "And in nothing terrified by your adversaries which is an evident token of perdition." The word "terrified" is rich and refers to a horse that cannot be used in the field because he has been spooked and frightened. Basically, the apostle says to never let your fear cause you to lose faith. Do not be so frightened that your faith cannot kick in and see you through. He uses the word "adversaries" to describe the people who are against you. The latter phrase "evident token of perdition but to you of salvation and that of God," is a horrible translation in the King James Version. It should read like this, "which is a clear indication that you can easily be defeated and destroyed if you have not been saved and have the Lord on your side."

God allows Christians to have adversaries and

opposition. Okay, let me say the same thing another way. Everyone who smiles in your face is not your friend. Everyone you think wants you to succeed does not. But the question is, why? Here is the answer. God allows opposition so that you can have something to overcome. If you have nothing to overcome, it means you have no opposition; but when you have opposition God will always stand with you until your test of opposition becomes your testimony of total victory.

In 1 Samuel 17 there is a narrative recorded of David in a battle against Goliath from Gath. He is a giant that stands nearly ten feet tall. The armies of Israel were afraid of him, but while in the midst of making a lunch run to take his older brothers a bite to eat, David notices that this giant was taunting the armies of God. He volunteers for battle because he knows that God is on his side. He takes a rock and a slingshot, hits Goliath in the head, and the rest is history. Yes, David had opposition but God gave him the strength to overcome.

Howard was diagnosed with prostate cancer in the fall of 2003. It was a shock to him and his entire family. At first, he thought that it was all over. He had thoughts that his death would be immediate. He was filled with fear. Things seemed too much for him to handle. However, one day while in a chemo treatment, he heard the voice of God simply say, "I am with you." From that moment, he stopped having thoughts of his death and started planning how he would live each day of his life. He is more alive today than he has ever been. His giant was cancer, but he got prepared for battle, and now he has the testimony of a conqueror simply because he was fearless with the Lord on his side.

• • •

Faithful in Calamity

For unto you it is given in the behalf of Christ, not only to believe on him but also to suffer for his sake; Having the same conflict which ye saw in me, and now hear to be in me.

Phil. 1:29–30

Not long ago, my son Jonathan and I went to pick up dinner for my wife and daughter. It was our day to treat, so we headed to pick up some food from a nearby eatery that we love. However, when we got into the truck, my son noticed a bug on my windshield. He asked me to get it off, and I said, "Son, we will let the wind blow him away." We started down the street and the bug held on. We drove to the freeway, and he held on. We got onto the freeway, and he held on. We got off of the freeway, and guess what? He was still holding on. That little green bug held on until we got home, and then, on his own will, he flew away. You see, in spite of all of the wind, he held on. I discovered later from an Internet web page that the reason why that little bug could hold on so well was because God made him in such a way that he is designed to hold on when the strong winds blow. Now, if God could equip a little green bug that well, just think of what he has equipped you to do!

We live in an age that has been characterized by Christians who never suffer, but please understand that the best of saints suffer. The difference between the believer and the non-believer is character. Real Christians, in the face of the strong winds of calamity, simply hold on.

Paul says you are going to suffer. In fact, the verse says, "For unto you it is given that we suffer for the sake of Christ." The chief idea here is that it is given. You do not have to ask for it. Suffering is a gift. The term is *charidzo*. The root word is grace. Get that! The grace of God provides it. Paul says, "You have to go through yours and I have to go through mine" (paraphrase, Philippians 1:29). It is a conflict. The word "conflict" refers to a Greek athlete who has to play hurt in order to win. It refers to one who has to live with a scar or walk with a limp but refuses to quit.

The more we suffer in the place of Christ, the more we are blessed for the sake of Christ!

Most Christians today want the blessings of the Lord, but we tend to shy away from the testing of the Lord. The real truth is that one tends to define the other. If you show me a saint who has endured great testing, I will also show you a servant who will soon see great blessing. It is the way of the Lord. In fact, often times a saint will suffer with the Lord because God wants to bless them. The Lord blesses them by allowing the spotlight of human suffering to be shown upon them. As heaven watches, the earth peeps, and hell waits for a complaint. The saint in suffering is trusted by God to remain faithful, regardless of the suffering and hurt that life has to offer.

The story of Job has always been one of my favorites. It is because when God needed a witness to stand for his goodness, he allowed Satan to put the spotlight on Job. It does not look like a blessing or feel like one. In fact, the story reveals the fact that Satan charged God with cosmic bribery and fraud. Satan tells the Lord that the reason why Job loves him so much is because God has paid him off and rigged the election. So, God allows suffering to take place. It is severe. Job suffers the loss of his family, the loss of his property, and the loss of his health. Yet, if you could interview Job, what comes from his mouth brings glory to almighty God. In simple terms, he declares, "I came here naked, and I am going to leave here naked. The Lord is the one that gave it to me, and I trust him. The Lord is the one that took it from me, and I still love him. Blessed be the name of the Lord!" Yes, he suffers, but when the story closes he gains what he lost without losing the favor of the Lord.

Not long ago, while in flight from Houston to Chicago, I perused my way through a *Golf Digest*

Magazine. While flipping and reading the articles, hoping to find something to give aid and assistance to my horrid golf game, I stumbled across an article that gave strength to my faith. It was an article that gave a brief history of golf balls. I almost passed it up because the problem with my game is not the ball, it is everything else. However, to my amazement I found that when the golf ball was first invented its design was smooth. Yes, there were no bumps or dents on the surface. However, through research and years of study they discovered that a golf ball would fly much farther if it were dented. You see—the dent is to the golf ball what suffering is to the saint. All true believers have some dents. It is the trademark of true Christianity. They have been permitted by God to bless us. Yes, we suffer with Christ now but one of these days we will fly high with him. How high you ask? The Bible says that we shall be resurrected with him (Romans 8:17; 1 Peter 4:12). Now, that's great news! Suffering happens, and it may even cause some weeping, but when we are faithful, our course of weeping becomes the force of our joy.

The Spartans were prepared for battle and stood strong. Leonidas and his 300 men withstood the vast Persian army because they were prepared for battle. The question of the year is—how will you stand in days to come? If you are still alive and exist in time, you still have some fighting to do. But here is how you win and gain victory: Get prepared to do battle!

Refuse to be defeated, stand with the Lord of Hosts, the King of kings, and the Lord of lords. For us, he is Jesus Christ, Son of the living God, the promised Messiah, the Word made flesh, and our resurrected Savior. He will see you through!

listen|imagine|view|experience

AUDIO BOOK DOWNLOAD INCLUDED WITH THIS BOOK!

In your hands you hold a complete digital entertainment package. Besides purchasing the paper version of this book, this book includes a free download of the audio version of this book. Simply use the code listed below when visiting our website. Once downloaded to your computer, you can listen to the book through your computer's speakers, burn it to an audio CD or save the file to your portable music device (such as Apple's popular iPod) and listen on the go!

How to get your free audio book digital download:

1. Visit www.tatepublishing.com and click on the e|LIVE logo on the home page.
2. Enter the following coupon code:
   422e-f995-4b43-88c5-eac9-35bf-857d-e793
3. Download the audio book from your e|LIVE digital locker and begin enjoying your new digital entertainment package today!